The Grand Design - I
Reflections of a soul/oversoul

PADDY MCMAHON

Copyright © 2015 Paddy McMahon

www.paddymcmahon.com

All rights reserved.

ISBN-10: 1512018074
ISBN-13: 978-1512018073

Sooner or later questions such as "Who/and what am I? Where did I come from? How can I find meaning in my life? How can I reduce the pain of self-realisation? What will happen to me when I die?" begin to niggle at each of us. This book provides answers that come from a spirit being named SHEBAKA.

The Grand Design books, of which there are five volumes, explore life in all its aspects both in the physical world and in spirit. Inter alia, they explain how we came to inhabit physical bodies and what happens to us when we die; and they provide facts, concepts and suggestions designed to help us, in cooperation with our guides/guardian angels if we so wish, to find ever increasing happiness and fulfilment in our expression.

CONTENTS

Preface	1
Introduction	6
Light	8
Simplicity	10
Conscious and Subconscious – I	11
Man and God: Religion	13
Reincarnation	15
Guides (Guardian Angels) – I	17
Freedom	21
God	25
Prayer – I	31
Free Will	36
"Who made the World?"	40
The Stages of Evolutionary Growth	45
Awareness	68
Prayer – II	70
Appearance – Higher States	73
Good and Evil	75
Fear	78
Charity	80
Sin and Karma	83
Change	86
Conscious and Subconscious – II: Hypnosis; Dreams	90
Meditation: The Material and The Spiritual	94
Random Thoughts	98
Guides – II	99
Conclusion	104
About Paddy McMahon	105

PREFACE

My original intention was to let the material in this book stand on its own and not to bother with an introduction. In fact, I had in mind just to get it all written down and then to leave it among my confusion of papers and, perhaps, sometime after I had passed on somebody might find it and consider it worth sharing with others. Among other things, I felt that this would be a test of the genuineness of the material; if it had a significance for the public generally a way would be found to put it before them.

For a while I felt good about that approach. From my point of view it had a beautiful and, I now realise, egotistical simplicity. Above all else, it had the great merit, for me, that I didn't have to submit myself to the public in any way or risk changing the perception that I thought people who knew me might have of me. It was one thing to be an internal radical - in other words, in my own thoughts - but to be a public radical was something I shrank from. I also didn't want to be classified as a "nut". Most people who know me would, I'm sure, regard me as a conservative and definitely sane sort of person, fitting in pretty well with, and subscribing to, the established order of things, wanting no more than to live a quiet, orderly, comfortably anonymous life; so why would I want to change all that?

Ultimately, I think, the answer for me lies in the fact that I'm part of the jigsaw of the All, or God, or whatever word can be used to describe totality. I don't exist in isolation. As a spiritual being, by my very existence I'm eternally creative. If my life on earth is to mean anything I must contribute to the evolutionary and creative process in the best way I can. It seems to me, therefore, that, in a sense, it would be a denial of my existence if I deliberately refrained from sharing with others knowledge/wisdom/guidance which for some reason I have been privileged to have been given and which I have found indescribably helpful In my own life.

The question of responsibility arises in a double sense. First, much of what is contained in the book cuts across orthodox teaching. What if reading the book destroys somebody's faith? (e.g., in religion.) Second, how can I be sure beyond all doubt that the material in the book was transmitted to me from a highly-evolved source, as claimed, and was not a product of my own imagination? Facilely, I suppose I could say that if reading the book were to destroy somebody's faith then that faith didn't have a strong foundation anyway. Ultimately, though, I have to say that once I accept the line of thinking in the book for myself all I can do is offer that to other people. If they accept it, or partly accept it, or if some aspects of it cause them to question their own beliefs, then that's fine. If nothing like that happens for them, if they reject it totally, that's fine, too. In the final analysis each person has to take responsibility for himself.

On the question of the source of the material as well as the material itself the simple and honest answer is that I can't be sure beyond all doubt that what is claimed to be so is so. Yet I have very many proofs of guidance in line with what's contained in the book. I wouldn't regard myself as being abnormally perceptive; in fact, I doubt if I'm more than averagely so. Yet when I ask for guidance I am able to tell people (who request me to do so) many things about themselves, their past experiences, their families, their difficulties, even their future, So far, these have mostly been people with whom I had had no previous contact nor would I be likely to have in my own day-to-day sphere of activity; accordingly, I had no means from my own knowledge of them of being able to tell them what I told them - which has been almost invariably accurate. I can't really explain how this process (which, I suppose, comes under the category of clairvoyance) happens, other than to say that I know, beyond doubt, when it's happening and when it's not. I have, of course, considered all the obvious possibilities, such as telepathy, the subconscious, suggestion, but they all fall down when confronted with the fact that if I could operate in any of these ways I'd be able to do it all the time, not just on isolated occasions, A woman asked me once, "How do I know you're not reading my mind?" Yet nothing could have been further from her mind - her conscious mind, at least - than many of the things I had told her.

I think it is probably true to say that we live in an age where we tend to accept only what we can see before us except those things which we are already conditioned to accept. For example, we accept that Australia exists even though most of us have never seen it except on film or on a map. More significantly, many of us accept profoundly mysterious things, such as the existence of God or the transformation of bread and wine into the body and blood of the Son of God during a ritualistic ceremony, even though we have no visual evidence whatever on which to base that acceptance. I don't see myself as being outside this behavioural pattern. Acceptance of the material in the book caused me quite a lot of soul-searching even though I had the advantage of fairly extensive proof of guidance. I had to examine all my previously-held beliefs and submit them to as rigorous a process of analysis as I could. I stripped myself to the best of my ability of all conditioning and got myself into a situation of suspended disbelief - in other words, of having no beliefs at all. Then I allowed my reasoning faculty (such as it is!) to take over. The net result is that I have come to accept unreservedly the line of thinking in the book - and, indeed, it is inconceivable to me now that, or how, I ever had any doubts. In the event, once I accepted the material through my reasoning faculty it became irrelevant for me whether the source was highly-evolved, as claimed, or not. For what it's worth, I believe and trust completely that the source is as claimed.

Incidentally, as I write this, I have no idea how or when the book is going to be published, but I know it will be published eventually. Since you are reading this, maybe you will take it as a proof that guidance works, that there is a grand design and that you and I and everybody else are all comprehended by it and, ultimately, freed by it or, more accurately, helped by it to free ourselves.

Paddy McMahon
December, 1984

At last publication is imminent. As its title implies, this is the first of a series of books which I hope it will be possible to publish later. The second book has already been written and the third started.

Paddy McMahon
February, 1987

Some years after I had completed and published the five volumes of The Grand Design I received a letter from a man asking me how did I intend to arrange for the continuing availability of the books after I passed on. I didn't really give the matter any consideration at the time as I trusted that, since Shebaka had overseen the production of the books, he would find a way to have the material in them preserved. My trust was reinforced by the fact some fifteen years after I had started this book I discovered that, in a physical incarnation, Shebaka had reigned as king of Egypt from 712 to 698 BC and, during an expedition, had discovered a scroll on which the story of creation according to the god Ptah was written. The scroll had been partially destroyed by worms. Shebaka arranged that the surviving part should be carved in stone in order to preserve it. (I described this in more detail in the chapter entitled More dialogue with Shebaka in book V of The Grand Design). I felt that it would be easier for Shebaka than it was in the physical lifetime to arrange things in his present celestial state!

At some stage in the 1990s, through my partner Maura, I had the good fortune to meet a young Armenian named Armen Sarkissian, who unexpectedly found himself working and living in Ireland and who I'm privileged to count as a close friend. Armen decided that I needed a website and, to my delight, he set one up and has continued to administer it, while refusing any recompense. As a computer engineer he is au fait with continuing technological developments and arranged to get some of my later books into eBook format. However, The Grand Design books presented a problem in that I hadn't been using a computer when I wrote and published them.

By a strange seeming coincidence (but, of course not so) I needed to telephone a friend Michael Sheridan over a matter that had nothing to do with computers. As we were finishing our conversation, Michael repeated an offer that he had previously made about getting my books into eBook format. Michael is a software engineer and a dream analyst. He had the equipment to enable the Grand Design books to be scanned and cooperated with Armen in getting all five books into eBook format.

The upshot of all that is that I can now answer the question posed way back by my correspondent. Thanks to three wonderful people, the books have transcended the physical limitations and uncertainty of printing and reprinting and have attained a sort of etheric immortality (more advanced than stone!).

Paddy McMahon
November, 2011

INTRODUCTION

9th October, 1981: At last I am come to send you greetings and to hope that we will have long and happy association. I am impressing my thoughts on your mind and you are converting them into your words. I will go slowly so that you will have time to put in your beloved punctuation marks!

I have let myself be called Shebaka because I know the sound of the name would have a certain appeal to you but in reality I have no name. I am coming to talk to you from a vibration where names are no longer important, where indeed communication is instantaneous and is so open that one communicates simply by being. Thus there is never any misunderstanding. I retain a memory of the circumstances of earth and I know the constraints they put on communication.

Why am I especially coming to communicate through you? Because this was part of our purpose, I should say is part of our purpose, that you would develop yourself to the stage where it would be possible for me to relay to you some of the wisdom to which it is my privilege to have access. You in your turn will find opportunities to pass on this distilled wisdom to others who may be interested.

I am no stuffy higher being, I just happen to be in a higher vibration. Nor do I want to set myself up as a know-all, nor as an object of veneration, nor as a symbol of sanctity. I only tell you about the higher vibration to reassure you and anybody else who might have access to these words that I speak with some authority having progressed through many stages of evolutionary growth. I will be talking about these stages later but if you want to think in terms of seven stages such as are already familiar to you then I come at present from the sixth stage. I am also in a position to describe the seventh stage.

Now I sent you the message last night to keep reading because I wanted and want to stress that all of what I might call your spiritual reading has been nudged in a certain direction and that I have been in the background keeping a "hooded eye" over the communications that have already come to you. Again I only mention this for reassurance.

It is not necessary to make an appointment for certain times to do this writing unless you want to do that. For me time does not exist in your terms, so it is up to you. I await your invitation whenever and wherever suits you. I can tune into your thoughts at any time and you are finding that you have no difficulty in tuning into mine.

It would be better to type these notes rather than the earlier ones. I will cover some of the earlier material again in any event.

LIGHT

12th October. If I don't use any form of salutation or greeting it is not that I don't wish to convey good wishes but that I want to convey the continuity of my contact. So you can take that for granted.

You would wish that our communication would be more obvious, maybe that I would show myself and sit opposite you while we're talking. It's not possible for me to do that at this stage. I am too far removed from the earth vibration to be able to assume its physical characteristics without a lot of preparation. So you'll have to take me on trust.

Today I would like very briefly to discuss the significance of light. You know it within its ordinary meaning as something by which you see, such as the light of day or electric light or even the light of understanding. There is of course also light meaning not heavy. But light in a spiritual sense means much more. It is illumination of the soul, of the whole being, so that ultimately all darkness is gone. Light spreads and eliminates (not illuminates, although that may come first) darkness. This is also tied in with vibration. The earth is a heavy vibration and so is the physical body which keeps the soul chained to that heaviness. At physical death the soul (or real being) leaves the heaviness behind and is no longer constrained by the limitations of that heaviness. It is feeling light as opposed to heavy although it has probably not yet eliminated the darkness of misunderstanding from its perceptions. It is a strange paradox that the assumption of heaviness (I use "heaviness" rather than "weight" as being more expressive of what I mean) as, for example, going through an earth experience may help to accelerate the process of becoming light - rather like going on a diet, I suppose! When Jesus talked about himself as being the light of the world he was using light in its widest meaning of full understanding, full acceptance, full freedom of spirit, not weighed down by any darkness of bigotry or intolerance or false pride or false humility or any restrictive emotion. "Let there be light" is the best wish that one can make on behalf of all. So a lot of what I will have to say in later sessions will be devoted to spreading light into dark corners.

SIMPLICITY

14th October. Today I want to talk about simplicity. There is no truer statement than that life is simple. The trouble is that human beings complicate it. (More than human beings do but my words are only addressed to human beings.) Take a rose, for instance, it buds and blooms, fades and passes on. Nothing could be simpler and nothing is more beautiful. The nature of being is as the rose. It is an unfolding of love. The bud symbolises the soul as yet unaware of its own beauty and magnitude. Then the blooming comes as light flows and represents the slow awakening of the soul to its destiny. The fading away is a physical happening which has the appearance of reality but is only an illusion. The inflow of light increases the awareness of love which in turn increases the possibility of simplicity. God is love. We are all part of God. We are love. Nothing could be more simple. It's only when human beings forget who and what they are that complications arise.

CONSCIOUS AND SUBCONSCIOUS – I

16th October: The distinction between the conscious and the subconscious mind is generally a source of much confusion. Where does consciousness end and subconsciousness begin? And, most importantly, where does the subconscious end? Am I talking to you now or are you just using your subconscious mind?

It will be easier if I start with the last question first. You are conscious. You are aware of where you are, what you're doing, what's going on around you. Your mind is working normally. The only abnormal thing is that thoughts are flowing through from what you believe to be an external source, you are converting them into words and writing them down.

Consideration of this question is central to the whole business of spirit communication, spirit guidance, guardian angels (I shouldn't describe them as a business!), inspiration from whatever source. Creativity of any kind is involved; is the inspiration coming from the subconscious to the conscious mind or is there any external guidance? I know I'm talking to you and you know I am. But who am I? Am I your subconscious, part of your subconscious, your higher self (or lower self!), or a separate individual? I am both part of you and separate. We are all part of God and God is a unity. Therefore we are all part of each other. At the same time we each have our own individuality. It's like a jigsaw puzzle - although this is a limited analogy. No two parts are the same and each part is indispensable to the whole. (Why the analogy of the jigsaw is a limited one I will go into later but it serves for the purpose of illustration now.) You are an individual personality and I am a separate individual personality. When that is applied generally then, of course, it means that all the kinds of communication I referred to earlier may come from separate spirit sources.

What then is the subconscious? It's the inactive part of the mind, the storehouse of memories and information of all kinds. It's like a computer data bank. At the press of a button (a shock, an emotional experience) memories are let loose, old feelings triggered off, what has been repressed comes to the surface. The subconscious may be rather similar to a (minor) sleeping volcano which erupts on occasion pouring its lava in all directions. The more in balance a person is the less part the subconscious plays in his life. It is a mistake to think that any inspiration can come from the subconscious. It is no more capable of providing inspiration than a computer is and unfortunately it cannot be controlled in the same way as a computer. It is desirable for all that they should eliminate the subconscious altogether by increasing the power of the conscious mind. Consciousness ends when the conscious mind gives over control to the subconscious, for example, when it allows fears and anxieties to take over. And subconsciousness ends, of course, when the conscious mind takes over positive direction of a person's life. The only demons in existence are creatures of the subconscious. Eliminate the power of the subconscious, tune in to guidance and you will begin to appreciate the simplicity of life.

MAN AND GOD: RELIGION

Man and his relationship to God and the ways in which he has sought to know and express that relationship have been burning questions (often literally!) throughout the ages. The search for answers to these questions has led to the foundation of religions and cults which have set themselves up as intermediate stations between God and man and have by and large purported to interpret for man the word and wishes of God.

In our earlier session today I referred to the fact that God is a unity and that we are all part of that unity each in an individual unique way. Since each of us is a part of God it follows that God is within each of us. That's what's meant by the words, "The kingdom of God is within you". God therefore is not and cannot be a remote being separate from us. I don't want to go further than that in this session as later I would like to give a separate session on God.

I don't wish to understate in any way the benefits and the divisions which religions have brought to mankind. They have at one and the same time provided great comfort to people in need of it and restriction of freedom on people least likely to be able to cope with restriction. They have given answers with great authority and sheltered people within the ambit of that authority. Conformity brings salvation, non-conformity may lead to damnation, all expressed in terms of eternity! That religions have encouraged, often imposed, desirable codes of behaviour between people cannot be denied any more than that they have also encouraged and often imposed penal codes on those not of their persuasion. Men bonded together in a common cause tend to behave with savagery, albeit sometimes of a polite kind, towards those who do not agree with them.

I am being deliberately direct because I don't want to run any risk of being misunderstood. A physical life on earth is a means by which a soul may gain experience which will help to raise its level of awareness of itself as a part of God. Religion may or may not be of assistance towards that end. If it is in any way a division between the soul and its recognition of its unity with God, then religion cannot but be detrimental to that soul's growth. While that, of course, is just my point of view, I must add (rather pompously) that I give it in the certainty of what I am.

REINCARNATION

19th October: I might as well discuss reincarnation now rather than later so that it can be fitted into the perspective of continuing life. It is a subject which has always been a source of fascination for some and is now of growing importance to many.

I don't want to get into an involved argument about time. As I indicated earlier my aim is to simplify. It's a difficult concept for a human being to understand time in terms of a continuing present rather than in the familiar terms of past, present and future. Both are valid concepts in their own way (in their own time, if you like!). If you think of time in a global sense put into the context of a world in the round you will get some idea as to how the two concepts can merge. Then the past and the future come together into a series of recurring presents although often looked at from different points of view or reacted to in different ways. The division of time into seconds, minutes, hours, days, weeks, months, seasons, years and so on with season running into season in regularly repeating patterns illustrates the concept of time unfolding in a framework of change yet recurring sameness. I'm sorry if this sounds complicated but it is necessary for me to try to get across the idea of time as a vast continuing process which is not limited in the way that earthly divisions and indeed the finality of limited earthly life-spans condition human beings to believe.

Reincarnation is a fact, that is, it is a fact that souls choose to repeat earth experiences as part of the process of spiritual development and even sometimes just because they want to relive certain experiences in physical bodies. There is no more mystery about the fact of reincarnation than there is about rosebushes repeating the growth of roses. In what I have said earlier about time there is an argument for saying that since all life is lived in a continuing present there can be no such thing as earth lives following each other in a linear time sequence.

It is not necessary, indeed it is undesirable, to concern ourselves with such an argument because the reality is that human beings have to live their lives within a linear time sequence-but at the same time it is highly desirable that in the larger context of spirit as opposed to physical existence they should be aware of an unlimited concept of time. A simple way of keeping this in mind is to remember that you are spirit temporarily limited by the constraints of existence within a physical body but that you have chosen the condition for a particular purpose and that the constraints are learning experiences.

So reincarnation is a fact of physical existence. Some souls choose to reincarnate more frequently than others. The number of physical incarnations which a soul may have had is no index to its progress in spiritual development. Reincarnation is only one way towards spiritual development; there are many others and some souls choose not to incarnate or reincarnate at all. This explains the often conflicting information coming from spirit sources about reincarnation. Some are simply not aware of it in the vibration in which they exist.

Because every soul has free will reincarnation can have positive and negative effects. On the positive side an earth life can be a particularly good developmental experience because there are so many challenges to be met, e.g. illness, poverty, wealth, conditioning. The soul that uses its environment positively will gain much. On the other hand, the soul that reacts negatively to its environment, e.g. becomes embittered, bigoted, intolerant or merely with passive acceptance of conditioning, may regress spiritually and will have to regain the lost ground subsequently.

I can't offer proof of reincarnation. I can only repeat that it is a fact.

After that it's a question of personal belief. It is well that all souls should be aware of the different possibilities of development, of which reincarnation is one.

GUIDES (GUARDIAN ANGELS) – I

19th – 20th October. I would like to elaborate on what I said earlier - in the session on 16th October about tuning in to guidance.

It's a strange thing that in all the centuries since human beings have inhabited the earth their understanding of life has largely stagnated. Their vision of life has rarely gone further than life on earth being a vale of tears to be succeeded by an eternity spent in adoration of a remote, patriarchal God with angels everywhere flapping their wings, or suffering horribly in a hell crowded with indescribably evil devils. That so many people have had and still have to live with such a vision of life and death is a great tragedy. Through the centuries many wise and developed souls have tried to open people's eyes to their own greatness as spirit beings but they have only succeeded in having themselves put on pedestals as saints or gods whereas what they wanted was that others should be given a chance to share their vision and find what they had found. The more developed a soul is the less it wants to be put on a pedestal and the more it reaches out with its whole being to help other souls to see what they are–the light I discussed earlier.

Now much is being done to spread among people the idea of continuity of life, not in the sense of judgment day and eternal heaven or hell but as a growth towards a realisation of each soul's integral unity with God. People are also being reintroduced to the idea that they have guardian angels, something which many believed and believe as children but which usually fades as the concept of angels assumes a fairytale or unreal image. Yet angels there are and each person, if he so chooses, has at least one assigned to him to guide him through his earth life. These angels are evolved souls who are familiar with earth's conditions and who have already learned the lessons it has to offer. The choice is made before the soul's entry or re-entry to earth. The soul has free will to decide whether it wants a guide or guides to help it. It is a matter of agreement between them. Even though they have other work to do guides are always available to the persons they have agreed to help; they are never more than a thought away. A person's free will is always sacrosanct. While the guides are constantly helping in all sorts of inspirational ways they will not interfere unless they are asked to do so.

It has been said that to know yourself is the beginning of wisdom. To know that you have guides to help you through life is a stepping-stone to wisdom. To tune in to your guides and to ask for their help is the achievement of wisdom. It would be a great mistake to think that in asking for help and advice from your guides in coping with the daily challenges of life you would in some way diminish yourself, or your capacity to make decisions for yourself. You cannot but increase your wisdom and decision-making capacity by reaching out towards a higher consciousness than your own. In a very real sense the more you tune in to guidance the more self-reliant you become because you begin to realise that you have immediate access to all the answers you need. Thus the living of life becomes a simple and enjoyable process. You are making the best possible decisions in harmony with the universal scheme of things and you know that you are doing exactly what you set out to do with your life.

People who choose to relive an earth experience for the sake of repeating a pleasurable sensation or series of sensations usually do not wish to have guides helping them. However, if at any stage during their earth lives they change their minds there are many evolved souls willing and only waiting to be asked to act as guides. For such is the universal love of which we are each a part that we are only being true to our own natures if we help each other. And in helping each other we also, of course, help ourselves. None of us exists independently of another which is often hard to accept in the daily commerce of living, particularly when a situation of antipathy arises between people.

I have talked about tuning in to guidance. How best can this be done?

The easiest way is to set aside a little time each day, a little time of stillness, for communication with your guides. This needn't be the same time each day, it needn't be any particular time of the day; but no matter how busy you are you should make a point of having a few quiet minutes of communication. If you have particular problems to solve or decisions to make meditate on them and ask your guides for their advice. Just wait for it - it will come, maybe in the form of words or a feeling or a picture - but it will come. With practice you will be able to do this automatically as often as you need to during the day.

How can you be sure that it's your guide or guides talking to you and not some less evolved or mischievous spirit? It is true that many souls do not wish to give up the influence they had on earth and seek to control people by suggesting certain courses of action to them. Or well–meaning relatives may wish to continue to shelter their children and loved ones from the challenges of life. But if you make a conscious decision to ask your guides for help they will see to it that no other spirit can communicate with you without invitation on your part. Remember that you make the decision. If you don't ask for their help the guides cannot impose themselves on you. This is the nature of love; it never seeks to possess or impose. There is no limit to the amount of help available to you; if there is a limit it will have been set by you.

Does all this mean that if you have a problem you can simply ask your guides to help you solve it or to offer you a solution? Yes, most certainly. Don't just take my word for it. Try it and see.

I have given a lot of attention to this session on guides and I will probably come back to it again in later sessions because I, in common with many others, feel that humanity as an experience will continue to stagnate unless it can be given positive direction from spirit. As I have emphasised, this can only be done with the conscious co-operation of those experiencing humanity. But what a marvellous world it would be if all were linked together in a co-operative effort stretching through all the stages of spiritual evolution.

In concluding this session I would like to draw attention to the traditional role given to angels, that of being messengers of God. And so they are, but they are more than that. They are the custodians of God in the centres of those whom they guide.

FREEDOM

22nd – 23rd October: There has been much written, much spoken and a lot of fighting over the notion of freedom. The right to freedom is usually regarded as a basic human right. But what is meant by freedom?

It can be safely said that slavery is usually regarded as the antithesis of freedom. It can also be safely said that a slave is not physically free. Slavery is no longer openly practised in a manner of buying and selling, yet it is still an inherent part of the human condition as it at present obtains. For example, marriage is a common human condition. People decide to get married for various reasons. Men and women have a natural mating instinct which can be satisfied most respectably in the prevailing social climate within the institution of marriage. There is a longing for security, for permanence, for communication on an intimate level, for perpetuation and for children (which may be partly the same thing), for protection, for readily available sexual experience, for conformity, for acceptance as an apparently well-adjusted member of society, or for any of a number of other things. I know I might be expected to mention love but it would, I think, be inaccurate to do so as it is highly improbable that the word love means the same thing to any two people. In any event, a marriage takes place and in due course it is likely that a child or children are born. For the sake of tradition let us say that the father is the breadwinner and the mother stays at home to mind the children and do the housework. As the years pass, the daily grind, in his case of travelling to and from work and getting little personal satisfaction from his work, and in her case of monotonous household tasks and perhaps the isolation of suburban existence and the demands of children, produce in middle and later years, if not earlier, a sense of futility, dissatisfaction and waste and, also, hopelessness at the impossibility of escaping from the burden that had been placed on them other than by dying, which is not a welcome alternative. Under all the frustration there's a feeling that life should have more to offer than this.

There's no point in trying to overlook the fact that the scenario I have described is a common feature of modern civilisation. I have taken the example of a married couple as being the most usual human condition. But, of course, many people who are not married exist under conditions which provide their own form of slavery. The person who spends many years caring for an aged parent, the religious struggling under a rule of celibacy, the child oppressed by the demands of school or the home environment, these are but some of many examples. Other forms of slavery are not exclusively confined to the married or single states; for example, alcoholism, gambling, cigarette-smoking, drug-taking, promiscuity, disability, illness, single-minded devotion to a cause. You may well ask - is there anybody at all in the human condition who is not a slave? What about you trying to put words on my thoughts? Devotion to a cause!

The only answer I can give is that a person is what he thinks. Not what he thinks he is—what he thinks. If you think positive, you are positive, if you think free, you are free. How about a person in prison—what good will it do him to think free? The only difference between a prisoner and anybody else is that his physical freedom to move is subject to more restrictions. But he is as free as he wants to be in his thoughts. What I am saying is that the only way a human being can be free is in his thoughts. Every physical human condition, without exception, is subject to restriction. But a person's thoughts are exclusively his own. He can share them with others or not as he wants. He may say that his thoughts are influenced by the physical conditions under which he lives; for example, how can he but think bitter thoughts if he is old and alone, abandoned by his family, and with only an old-age pension on which to house and feed himself? I can only say to him that it is his free choice whether he thinks bitter thoughts or not. But as he thinks, so he is. He thinks bitter thoughts, he is a bitter old man. He thinks joyful thoughts, he is a joyful old man. There are many instances of people who live under exactly similar physical conditions but who, because of the way they think, either rise above those conditions or allow themselves to be adversely affected by them.

Freedom in the real sense can never be a matter of nationalistic achievement or the right to self-government or to own property or to practise religion or to marry or to divorce or to vote or to act as you would wish to act at any given time. Those things constitute a physical licence within an always limited framework. Real freedom, however, is totally unlimited. It is a spiritual thing - which does not mean that all spirits, even those without physical bodies, are free. A spirit being with a physical body can achieve freedom as well as a spirit being without a physical body; the way to freedom for both is through their thoughts.

Ideally, then, a person should not limit himself by his thinking or, to put that in a positive way, he should free his thinking from all constraints. There are obvious constraints such as bigotry, hatred, bitterness, intolerance, anger, self-righteousness, fanaticism, despair, envy, but there are other less obvious ones such as piety, prudishness, holiness, self-denial, self-glorification, duty, guilt, impatience, anxiety, worry, fear, authoritarianism, desire to be loved, to be popular, to be wealthy, to be famous, to possess or to be possessed, to achieve power or position, to impose a code of behaviour or a particular viewpoint, to conform, to be seen as conventional, to be seen as respectable and respected, to uphold tradition, to be sexually attractive, to be sexually potent, to be recognised as a success, to be appreciated, to be praised, to be shown gratitude for favours done, to repay or be repaid debts, to punish, to harbour grievances, to seek happiness in people, places or things, to escape from a particular situation, to have job satisfaction, to have sexual satisfaction, to be able to buy better clothes or food or a more expensive house or car. It may not be an exhaustive list but it's an exhausting one! What I've been trying to show is that not only the obvious things but also what might be regarded as normal wishes and urges are all in their own way constraints on freedom, the real freedom of thought, and by their very existence in thought form they present a barrier which blocks off the receptiveness of the mind to other thoughts.

So what good is freedom, then, if it means giving up so much of what is normally regarded as pleasurable? Freedom doesn't mean giving up anything. It means being free of the pressure of anything and everything. It doesn't mean giving up the experiences of living. It means looking at them from a different perspective. It means giving rein to the unfettered joy of being, knowing that to be is everything. A spirit, part of God, does not need anything; it already has everything. It is free if it will but realise its freedom. The process of realisation is the often painful journey that all must travel. It is unfortunate that pain is involved but that it is the nature of spirit that all must ultimately be free is the supreme consolation. Part of the purpose of these sessions is to help to take the pain out of the journey towards realisation and to make it an enjoyable trip instead.

GOD

25th – 31st October: I said in an earlier session that I would like to devote a full session to God.

In talking about God I immediately run into the limitations of language. God is not a person so I cannot say "He" or "She". I don't want to use the word "It" either because it's not expressive enough. At the risk of being more than usually repetitive I'll use the word "God" where normally "He", "She" or "It" might suffice.

I have talked about each of us being a part of God, that is, the spirit beings that we are. So God is at least the sum total of the parts, like the analogy of the jigsaw I referred to in an earlier session. But God is more than the total of the parts which is why I said that the jigsaw was a limited analogy.

Somewhere at the back of your mind there's a memory of having been told that God had no beginning and will have no end. Everything in the physical earth plane points to beginnings and ends; day and night, sleeping and waking, birth and death. So the idea of infinity is alien to humanity and very difficult, if not impossible, for a human being to comprehend in all its grandeur. Yet, having said that, I have to go on to say that God is an infinity of spirit existing through infinity. In other words, God is not limited by any concept of time or space. Therefore we cannot think of God in terms of time or space or consequently beginning or end.

Then how did it all start - the world, etc.? In the sense that everything is contained in God everything has always been. God is eternally creative, however, so the structure or format of things keeps changing. Thus nothing ever dies but evolves into something else. All creation evolved out of God as an expression of the love that God is. Each part of creation is infused with that love and in turn expresses it in a creative way. That's easy enough to understand, I think. You can think of examples such as an artist, a writer, a carpenter, a cook, or anybody who ever writes a friendly letter or says a kind word to anybody else, or grass growing, a flower blooming, a bee making honey, a cat purring, a dog licking your face or wagging its tail, or water flowing, a spider building its web, or a bird its nest.

Of all our sessions this is the most difficult because I have to try to convey an understanding of the infinity of God in words which are themselves an expression of finite concepts. If you don't understand a word you look it up in a dictionary which gives its meaning in another word or other words; then the word has a meaning for you which is related to your own limited understanding or experience of what the other word or words convey. However, I've no business doing these sessions at all if I can't make myself understood in simple terms. At the same time I want to remind you that when communication is reduced to words unanimity as to the interpretation of the words is rarely achieved.

Enough posturing! The most comprehensive and I hope most comprehensible definition of God I can give is this: God is an infinity of spirit, who has existed and will continue to exist through infinity, who is the source of all creativity, who is the life force of all creation, whose inspirational creativity never ceases nor ever will cease, who cannot be contained or confined in any limited or finite idea such as a person, place or thing; all creation, and each bit of creation individually, is a part of God, but it cannot be said that God is the sum of all creation because that would be putting a limit to God and there is no limit; each part of God has a share in God's infinite creativity; above all else, God is love, infinite love.

Now I have come back to the word "love" which conveys so many different things to people. It's a much used and I suppose I could say much abused word. It's probably one of the most frequently used words of all. It's used in connection with a feeling a man may have for a woman or a woman for a man, which may be a thing of romance or of passion; or the feeling a person of one sex may have for a person of the same sex, which may have nothing to do with homosexuality or may indeed be a homosexual thing; or the feeling a parent may have for a child or a child for a parent; or the feeling friends may have for each other; or the feeling a person may have for an animal or an animal for a person; or the feeling a person may have for a possession, or an activity, or an experience; or the feeling a person may have for the God he envisages, or for a saint. It may be taken to mean anything from lust to ecstasy of a mystical kind. The wide variety of meaning given to it is a useful thing to bear in mind when you are trying to visualise the all-embracing concept of God. Every person has experienced and continues to experience love in different ways within the variety of meanings assigned to it. If a person says he loves someone or something he is giving expression to a feeling in a way that makes sense to him at a particular point in time.

When I say that God is love, then, what do I mean? I mean that God is the animating force in all expression which includes all life and all activities of life. I know what you're asking - surely not all activities of life - for example, wars, murders, oppression, rape, torture? Or the creation of an ugly-looking beast like a hippopotamus? Or irritating insects like fleas? Bear with me for a minute when I say that all life and all activities of life without exception are part of the positive expression of love. In other words, there is no evil. There is apparent evil and to human eyes many people act in such a way and many things are done which can only be described as bad or evil. For instance, how can I say to a mother whose daughter is raped that the man who performed the act of rape and the act of rape itself are animated by the force of love? Yet, that is the reality. Let me give you an example. A man and a woman meet, are attracted to each other and decide to get married. They have two children, a boy and a girl, both of whom they love very much. Time passes and the children grow up. The boy, now a young man, becomes part of a particular group who indulge in a lot of violent activities, including robbery and rape. The young man participates fully in the group's activities. In the meantime, his sister has channelled her life into a positive stream of respect and helpfulness towards all the people with whom she comes into contact. His parents are worried as a result of their son's behaviour. They remember him as an innocent child and they wonder where did they go wrong in his upbringing. They talk to him, pray for him, but apparently without success. They continue to love him even as he continues to reject them. In due course the father dies and some time later the mother also passes on. The son had lost all contact with them by this time. He is now much older and by his way of life he has become a coarse and brutal man. Much of his life is spent in recurring prison stretches. In the fullness of time he dies violently as he had lived. Meanwhile the remaining member of the family, his sister, had joined an order of nuns; she lived a most exemplary life and died surrounded by the love of her community.

On the face of it, three of the four people in that family unit were good people and lived positive lives. There is no difficulty in regarding them and their activities as animated by the force of love. The son, however, was apparently an evil man and performed evil deeds during most of his life on earth. The problem is to accept that both he and his activities were animated by the same force of love as his parents and sister.

If you get a bad boil in your leg the treatment will probably be to lance it and let all the badness out. Love operates in somewhat the same way. The son in my case history had, by the exercise of his free will, built up a reservoir of negativity within himself as a spirit being which the love that he was and is forced out of him during that particular lifetime. The same force of love operating within the recipients of his acts of violence righted by his acts an imbalance which earlier acts of free will on their part had created in them. He also helped his parents and his sister by creating in them because of their love for him a tolerance and a compassion which it would not be possible for them to feel had they not come up against the conflicts which he caused in them by the intimacy of his relationship with them. The very extent of his violence should in due course produce for him a remedial effect in a somewhat similar way to a sharp slap administered to an hysterical person. The old saying that things must get worse before they get better is very relevant in certain circumstances.

In the case history given there was a lesson to be learned for each of the four people involved. But if God (or love) is the animating force in every person and thing how come that the process of apparent evil ever became necessary, in other words, that love seems to express itself in a seemingly unloving way? Because contrast is necessary for a full appreciation of life. The person who has never experienced cold cannot fully appreciate heat. The person who has never been thirsty or hungry cannot fully appreciate drink or food. A landscape artist would find very little expression in his painting if there were no clouds or shadows to counterbalance or highlight clear skies and light. A playwright's work would be very dull if there were no conflict in it. If you didn't know the feeling of anger you couldn't fully appreciate the value of serenity. The people who have lived through a war are almost invariably the ones who treasure peace most. A person who has never experienced pain cannot reach a full appreciation of the state of freedom from pain. Life on earth is a learning experience designed to bring the person going through it to a fuller perception of the spirit being that he is. He is, in fact, undergoing a series of training courses geared to the raising of his awareness and consciousness levels. Because of his free will it is up to himself how he responds to the training. But the love within him, indeed the love that he is, will keep on throwing up situations and experiences until he has learned all the lessons he needs to learn to reach the full awareness of that love.

So then things aren't what they seem to be. It is well said that you should never judge the book by the cover.

Now the question asks itself - if all this is so, if all the bad as well as the good experiences of earth existence are part of a broad design of love operating to achieve awareness of itself, how did that same design of love ever allow the state of stunted awareness to come about? That's a big question and I'll have to devote a separate session to it so as not to let this session become too diffuse. I'll confine myself at this stage to saying that a certain number of individual souls - a segment of God, if you like - by the exercise of their free will allowed their awareness to become obscured to such an extent that in some cases it has seemed to become almost non-existent. (We're back to the poor hippopotamus and the flea again!) The force of love could not allow this to continue - it isn't possible for it to negate itself or any part of itself - and so began the long journey back to self-realisation. Some souls have still to start the journey, others have made it all the way back and the rest are at various stages in between.

Much of the teaching about God has centred on a divinity concentrated in three persons - Father, Son and Holy Spirit. As I have said, God cannot be identified in personal terms except in the sense that God is present in all persons. Therefore God cannot be confined to three persons unless they are seen as representing all life. I would suggest that it would be very helpful to use the symbolism of the Father in terms of those souls who never lost or who have regained their self-awareness, the Son in terms of those souls who are still at the start of the journey or who have still not mastered the lessons of earth, and the Holy Spirit in terms of those souls who have evolved beyond the lessons of earth and who are helping others to find their way, for example, spiritual helpers or guides or guardian angels, whatever you wish to call them. In this way the chain of co-operation running through all life can be easily seen.

PRAYER – I

2nd – 4th November. Since I talked about God in the last session it's logical that this one should be about prayer.

Prayer is, I think, accepted to mean a form of address to God or to some saintly being who is regarded as an intermediary to God. The address is usually couched in formal terms in a format which is in general usage, although, of course, this is not necessarily so.

As a rule it's probably true to say that prayer combines worship of God with specific requests for certain favours. The person praying usually does so in a supplicatory way, on his knees, often with head bowed and hands joined.

The history of mankind shows that prayer to a deity of some kind has been common practice. People have always felt the need for a higher power to regulate the flow of their lives. At times of crisis the need is intensified.

It's a widespread custom for people to pray for their deceased relatives, usually for the happy repose of their souls.

Now I'd like you to consider prayer in the context of the concept of God I outlined in our last session. Remember that the person praying is a part of God and therefore an infinity of spirit in his own right. In that light it is meaningless, for instance, to pray for the happy repose of a soul since it is in the nature of the soul to be on its eternally creative way; the last thing it needs is repose in the sense requested.

Suppose you are a father or a mother. One of your children kneels in front of you with head bowed and begs you for a new bicycle. What's your reaction? You're not happy about the child kneeling in front of you and explain that it's not necessary to do so and that you would prefer if he just came to you in a straightforward way with his request. You go on to consider whether it would be wise for him to have a bicycle just now and, if so, whether you can afford to buy it.

Now let's suppose that the child, instead of going to you, goes into a church or kneels down beside his bed and prays to God for a new bicycle. His prayer is heard by his guide (or guides) who applies the same yardstick to it as the father or mother in the previous example. If it seems to be in the child's best interests to have a bicycle the guide will be able to set up a set of circumstances by which one will be made available for him.

In the first example, of course, the child would not have knelt before his father or mother; he'd just simply have asked for the bicycle. Wouldn't it be a much more simple and dignified arrangement if he did the same in the second instance? It would make his guides so much happier if he was aware enough to know about their existence and that they were most eager and anxious to help him.

The drawback with prayer as commonly practised is that it's a debasing ritual addressed to a remote personal God who doesn't exist in those terms. The prayers are still heard, yes, as in the example given above and sometimes it's possible to answer them in a practical way, but, generally speaking, they do nothing to heighten the level of self-awareness of the people praying. The gulf in spirit remains unbridged. That's why I place so much importance in regular day-to-day communication with guides. They can give so much help to people, if they are asked to do so, not alone in meeting the daily challenges of life but in finding meaning in them which is ultimately the only value in having to meet them.

As already explained, life on earth is a learning experience and to be of any value has to consist of a series of challenges many of which are painful to meet. The learning experience can, however, be enjoyable and life can follow a simple pattern if people tune in to their guides and ask for help in coping with and learning from each daily situation. That's prayer made easy and effective.

Apart from the more mundane daily needs prayers are said for more global needs such as peace or unity. There's absolutely no point in praying for these things. They're already available within yourselves if you will only open your awareness to them.

Communication on what I might describe as a conversational level with your guides is one effective form of prayer. Another which I recommend as a big help towards increasing self-awareness is meditation on unity with the Father, with the Father symbolising those souls who have never lost or who have regained their self-awareness.

This is the ultimate goal which all must reach. If you meditate on it regularly you will find it a very rewarding experience. I suggest that you include your guides in the meditation so that it becomes a joint venture. Apart from the bonding effect, this will greatly help your self-awareness or your growth in self-awareness. If you want to verbalise in order to help your concentration you can use a form such as, "We and the Father are one" and let that serve as the basis of your meditation. After a while you won't need any words.

Repetition of the same words and phrases over and over again is inevitably likely to become a mindless ritual for many people and while it may have value as a form of consolation or hypnosis or self-hypnosis it is not, in my view, helpful insofar as growth in awareness is concerned.

I'm sorry if I'm being very blunt in this session but, as I said earlier, I'm trying to take the pain out of the journey towards self-awareness. To my mind prayer as commonly practised is a form of mental and physical torture and is an abnegation of spirit. Constant communication with guides on a basis of mutual respect and spiritual equality with a recognition that the guides have reached a higher state of consciousness than the person being guided and wish to bring him up to that level, plus meditation on unity with the Father, again shared with the guides, will enable a joyful unfolding of spirit without any pressure of usage or form or ritual.

You have questions.

How does my statement in the session on God to the effect that all activities in human existence without exception are animated by the force of love tie in with saying that prayer as commonly practised is of no value spiritually? There's no contradiction. Many activities that people engage in carry no spiritual significance in themselves - for example, doing crossword puzzles or looking at a football match - but the people themselves are spirit beings, part of God, and that very fact invests the activities with the force of love. Such activities are generally recognised as being pleasurable (usually!) pastimes and no more than that and the people are not fooling themselves that what they're doing has spiritual importance.

What about prayers for the development of those who have passed on from earth? Their own guides and other souls will, of course, be available to help them in any event. If the soul is not prepared to ask for, or accept help, all the prayers in the world won't do any good. In fact they will only achieve an increase of earthbound pressure on the soul and thus hinder rather than help its progress. The best thing to do is to ask your guides to help the soul in whatever way they can. Your concern for the soul, if conveyed to it at the right time and in the best way, may well inspire it to seek help. Your intervention in this way could be very helpful particularly if the soul concerned has a high regard for you.

By putting the matter in the hands of your guides you allow for the use of discretion in approaching the soul concerned. Just think for a minute - isn't it a strange presumption that the God who is supposed to be all - knowing and all-loving needs to be prayed to in order to provide help for a soul which He (I'm using the usual terminology here) loves and knows is in need of help? Help cannot be imposed from outside. The soul has to make a conscious act of will to seek help. That's often the tragedy but ultimately the beauty of life.

Remember that in the symbolism which I already suggested if you are communicating with your guides you are communicating with the Holy Spirit. What more powerful form of communication could you have? And why make life complicated for people by imposing liturgies and ceremonies and rituals on them when they have the most effective possible answer to all their needs available to them in the simplest imaginable way?

FREE WILL

5th – 10th November. Free will is at one and the same time an integral and most precious attribute of spirit and the main obstacle to the achievement by the individual soul of full awareness of itself.

The nature of God (or love) is such that there can never be any question of imposition of will by a soul who has reached self-awareness upon another soul.

When expression evolved out of God into individual parts each part retained the full freedom of spirit which it always had. There was no such thing as reporting back to some superior being looking for permission to do this or that or the other; it was completely free to express itself in any way it chose. This is still the position and will always continue to be so; it cannot be otherwise.

I have already said that all must eventually return to a state of full awareness. This sounds more like predestination than free will. It is predestination in the sense, but only in the sense, that love cannot negate itself or any part of itself. A soul cannot be other than what it is, a spirit being, part of God, but it is entirely free to operate in any way it chooses. Free will is a matter of operation, not of being.

Take an example of a man who has a decision to make. He can choose one of a number of different options. The choice he makes may affect the way he lives his life and colour his thinking but he is still basically the same person. That's the way free will operates. The soul, the essential being, remains unchanged but its awareness level is affected by every act of free will.

If a soul by an accumulation of acts of free will reaches a certain level of awareness and decides, again by an act of free will, that it will remain at that level for ever how can I reconcile that with my statement that all must eventually return to a state of full awareness? The soul is, of course, free to make that decision and it remains at the level of awareness which it has chosen until it opts to move out of it. In practice, of course, no soul exists in isolation from all others. Sooner or later a decision to move is inevitable. The influence of love within the soul, the essence of its being, will continue to throw up experiences and guidance which will eventually help it to raise its level of awareness; the length of time this takes will be a result of the operation of the soul's free will in making its choices or decisions.

Have I made myself clear? The soul is; it has free will. I hope you can understand the distinction.

Respect for each soul's free will is an essential ingredient of spiritual development. Imposition or attempted imposition of will by one person on another or by a group of people on a person or people is a common feature of human existence and is one of the reasons why life on earth is such a valuable learning experience from the spiritual point of view. Obvious examples are: wars, physical force, threats, torture, laws, religious obligations, supervisory control, armies, police, courts, politicians, civil servants, parents, teachers, religious leaders. The less obvious ones may be more interesting, such as: persuasion, hinting, pleading, feigning illness or incapacity of some kind, playing on illness or incapacity, nagging, conferring or withholding of sexual favours, acting the martyr, praying for somebody without his consent, letting him know about the prayers, using any form of mind control without the agreement of the person concerned, tradition, conformity, outward show, shame, withdrawal, sulkiness, boredom, sincere belief in certain codes of behaviour or religious practices, perception of duty, skill, experience, sincere desire to help, faith, conviction that one knows what's best for another, lying, selectivity in argument or imparting information, reward, disciplinary measures, promises, creation of expectations, mystery, uncertainty, dependence, possessiveness, fear of not being accepted, insecurity, times of crisis.

Suppose a child decides that he would like to run over a cliff. The father sees that the child will be killed or badly injured if he doesn't intervene. So he stops him; an apparently clear-cut case of the father imposing his will on that of the child.

I said at the beginning of this session that the nature of God (or love) is such that there can never be any question of imposition of will by a soul who has reached self-awareness upon another soul. Where does that leave the father in the example given above? The child is not in a position to exercise choice. While he is a soul spiritually equal to his parents he has chosen to place himself in his physical environment for a brief period of time under their care - with their agreement, of course. The child, as spirit, would not be damaged by running over the cliff, but his physical body would. In his present state he is not aware of this. By his own choice, an act of free will, he has given his parents the right to exercise his free will on his behalf until he has become sufficiently aware of physical conditions to do it for himself.

Take another example. You are walking by a river and you see a woman about to throw herself into a particularly deep spot apparently with the intention of committing suicide. Do you stop her? If you do, aren't you showing disrespect for her free will? The answers here are no, if you have reached a state of full awareness, and yes. Remember that the woman is an indestructible spirit. By her act of physical destruction of her body she may well create a condition for herself which will ultimately help her to raise her awareness level. You are not likely to do her any favour in the long run by interfering, hard as that may be to accept if viewed from a physical or limited spiritual perspective.

You want to know what would be the position in the first example if the adult on the scene was not a parent of the child? The same. The adult would be in the place of the parent. The difference between the two examples is that in the first the child is not aware of what he's doing, in the second the woman is. If, on the way down to the water or when she is in the water, the woman cries out for help the picture is changed. She has now exercised her free will in a different direction. If you save her physically in that situation the effect on her awareness is likely to be far better than if you save her against her will before she jumps.

What about the position of parents insofar as the practice of religion by a child is concerned? The parents sincerely believe that it is in the best interests of the child to have the support of religious belief and religious practice, but the child finds it all too boring for words and will only practise under duress. The parents hope that habit will eventually create interest. This is, of course, a common situation and is an example of lack of respect for free will. Of what possible spiritual benefit can it be to anybody - child or adult - to be forced to take part physically in a ritual which has no meaning for him? This type of situation has caused more spiritual stagnation than any other.

If you feel you have found something in the spiritual field which has brought great joy to you, you naturally want to share it with everybody. How you share is the biggest test you will ever have of your growing awareness. If you are really aware you will never seek to impose your beliefs in any way, either directly or indirectly, nor will you ever seek to convince others of the rightness or truth of those beliefs. The best you can do, and believe me it is the very best, is to make people aware of your beliefs in the most unobtrusive possible way when suitable opportunities, such as expressions of interest, present themselves.

In conclusion, I must apply what I have said to these sessions. With your agreement and co-operation they are being presented in written form so that people will be free to read them or not as they think fit. Needless to say, acceptance of some or all or none of what's in the sessions is entirely an exercise of free will on the part of the reader. Whether you put an exclamation mark at the end of the last sentence is entirely an exercise of free will on your part!

"WHO MADE THE WORLD?"

16th – 19th November: It's a simple but rather unsatisfying answer to give to somebody asking, "Who made the world?" to say that God did and after that to depend on mystery or faith for further answers.

You have seen it postulated that dinosaurs dominated the earth for 140 million years and that they became extinct about 65 million years ago. So the world is a pretty old place on that evidence.

In this session I would like to convey as simply as I can why and how the physical world came into existence. I'm not going to go into scientific explanations, I'm merely going to state the facts in a bald sort of way.

First of all, I'll have to repeat myself a little. God is love. Expression evolved out of love into individual parts each with full free will. The process of evolution is within a time sequence in your terms and I'll explain it on that basis although I would just mention again that time does not exist in the real world of spirit. However, in the physical world you operate within a time frame and that's your reality while you're there so there's no point in giving you details in a way that doesn't fit your concept of reality.

Over a million billion years ago (with a billion equalling a million millions; so long ago that there's no point in trying to put a time scale on it) the evolution into individual parts that I mentioned above happened. Each part, or soul, was spiritually equal to every other soul - each was equally endowed with the spirit of God (or love). The number of souls who thus evolved was a billion billion billions (with a billion again equalling a million millions). I promised in our first session that I would go into the various evolutionary stages or vibrations later and when I do I will try to convey a picture of what these souls were doing then and what most of them are still doing now in the state of full awareness. All were, of course, initially in that state.

Some billions of years after the expression into individual souls happened one soul decided that he would like to run the whole operation. In other words, he wanted to impose his will on all the other souls. During a period of about 50,000 years he managed to get the support of roughly 1% of all souls - which was a small proportion, but a lot of souls - in his quest for dominance; they were prepared to subordinate their wills to his. (Incidentally you can see now that the proportion used by Jesus when he talked about there being more joy in heaven over one soul who was lost being found than over ninety-nine already saved - or words to that effect - was not a randomly chosen one.) He has been commonly known as Lucifer. He drew around him an inner circle, each of whom in turn formed his own inner circle, and so on, so that within a relatively short period of time he had established a hierarchy of which he was the head. This development was entirely incompatible with the true nature of spirit but it's an interesting pointer to the importance of free will in the scheme of things. Lucifer by his desire for power used his free will to influence others; they of their own free will allowed themselves to be influenced; at the same time others who had not allowed themselves to be influenced were unable to interfere because of their respect for free will.

When Lucifer found that he couldn't extend his influence any further he decided that he would isolate himself with his supporters from the others. It will hardly come as a surprise to you to learn that there was no great battle of the heavens. Again, this would, of course, have been incompatible with respect for free will.

Once respect for free will was breached in Lucifer's case and in the case of all his supporters (who didn't respect their own free will in allowing it to become subordinate to his) there seemed to be nothing to stop it being breached again and again. Eventually the stage was reached where some souls had lost all awareness of their real selves and had become like zombies.

The souls who had not allowed themselves to be influenced by Lucifer observed with great concern what was happening. The link of love running through all spirit meant that what was happening to one was happening to all. Out of that concern evolved the world as a system which would provide a means by which lost souls could regain their awareness. In talking about the world I mean the whole universe - sun, moon, stars, planets, including earth. Existence on earth is only one of many learning experiences provided for souls.

Everything on earth is infused with love; for instance, grass, water, stones; but such things aren't souls. They evolved in the earth scene to help sustain life in physical form so that souls could stay in the earth vibration.

Life on earth can be categorised into two forms, stationary - in the sense of not capable of moving around - and non-stationary. Stationary life includes plants, trees, grass, flowers. Non-stationary life includes birds, insects, fish, animals, human beings. Stationary life, while animated by love, is not soul. Non-stationary life is.

That brings me to the dinosaurs and other life of that kind. I mentioned that many souls had lost all their awareness of their real selves. They were literally lost. The spirit of love operating through the souls who had not lost their awareness developed a design of existence on earth related to the state of awareness or non-awareness of souls at a particular point in time; hence the proliferation of insect, bird, fish, animal life. It's all a progression through to man which is the highest state of awareness (although often not obviously so!) on the earth plane.

But what of Lucifer? He had already lost self-awareness by his desire for dominance. The negative progression or regression continued in his case until he too was caught up in the general loss of identity. It is entirely mistaken to think of him as a prince of devils seeking to win over any souls he can to his kingdom of hell. He is as much a part of God as any other soul - he just simply lost his awareness of who and what he was. He has long since regained his lost position and he is now truly a bearer of light to those who are still in need of it.

I referred to non-stationary life being soul. If I may I'll again take the example of the hippopotamus and the flea. Each of these has lost all awareness of its real self. It's a strange and probably repulsive idea to think of a soul being housed in the body of a flea, not to mention that of a hippopotamus. Traditional teaching in western countries is generally to the effect that only human beings have souls (as distinct from being souls). That's not correct.

But, you say, think of all the millions and millions of insects alone - how could each one be a soul? Here's where we come up against another complication. There was nothing to stop individual souls from expressing themselves into parts in the same way as did God. This didn't happen with the souls who never lost their awareness precisely because they hadn't lost their awareness - they saw the total grand design of love and wouldn't interfere with it. But it did happen with the other 1% some of whom saw it as a means of increasing their numbers until eventually they would outnumber the 99%. So they evolved into parts, and the parts in turn evolved into parts, and so on. At this stage the original souls were already in a state of diminished awareness. The process of diminution was intensified as the parts multiplied until some reached the point of no awareness at all. Thus you might have millions of fleas who house parts of one original soul, the soul comprising the whole lot. It wouldn't be accurate to call this a group soul; it's one soul which diffused itself into millions of parts. As awareness increases the parts begin to reintegrate until eventually the complete soul is ready to experience existence housed in a human body.

That's the broad pattern which I have outlined as simply as I can. I was one of the 1%, so were you, so were all the souls who have been through an earth experience and others who have not, and so were the dinosaurs! It's hard to believe that we were so foolish - but we were. I have been fortunate enough to have found my way back to full awareness and now that I know the joy of it again it is my dearest wish that all the others of the 1% should regain their original state as quickly as possible.

How many of the 1% have already got back? It's a long process and not many have yet made it all the way but roughly half are well on the way.

Could it all happen again? Yes, of course, given free will. I think, however, that the experience of the 1% will be enough to prevent a repeat performance.

THE STAGES OF EVOLUTIONARY GROWTH

28th November – 27th December: What do I do to occupy my time? Well, I'm free of all pressure to occupy myself in any way and, as I said, time doesn't exist in this vibration.

The best thing I can do, probably, is to go through the different stages of evolutionary growth, as I promised in our first session.

I mentioned in the last session that the 99% designed a pattern of evolution to help the 1% recover their lost awareness. This pattern may be broadly banded into seven stages with the seventh being that of full awareness. Within each of the other six stages there are many states of growth with movement through the different forms of non-human life representing progress in increasing awareness.

The first stage is the lowest stage of awareness. All non-integrated souls, parts of souls if you like, whether they are temporarily housed in physical bodies or are in spirit form, are at this stage.

The second stage includes the human state. Souls are once again integrated. They have not yet learned all the lessons which earth existence or existence elsewhere can provide for them.

The third stage is one of appraisal or reappraisal where all the experiences the soul has acquired are evaluated. This is more a stage of reflection than of movement.

The fourth stage represents a considerable growth in awareness.
Souls who have reached this stage do not, for instance, have any further lessons to learn from earth existence. The guides are at this stage.

The fifth stage again includes much reflection and evaluation.

The sixth stage is one of great joy. The soul at last comes to know the full measure of what it had lost and has now found again. Before a soul leaves the sixth stage it will, of course, have regained full awareness so that it can enter the seventh stage.

Now I'll try to outline what happens at each of the stages.

The First Stage

How does a soul which has diffused itself into a million parts and lost all awareness of itself in the process begin to become aware? How can it help it to be expressed in physical existence as a million fleas? Insects survive by contact with other forms of life. Each one achieves some awareness even to a minute extent of something outside itself. For instance, a flea finds that it can feed off a human being! That little spark of awareness multiplied a million times may be enough to make it helpful for the soul to reincarnate in some other multiple physical species, such as mice. The idea is that with each incarnation awareness will increase. Initially the spur to awareness is purely the need for physical survival. Experiences eventually begin to raise the consciousness level until the soul reaches the point where it can see itself as an integrity.

The operation of free will has become suspended at this stage. Here the purpose of the grand design of evolutionary growth is to get the soul back to a state where it will once again be capable of exercising free will. As I have already said the grand design was brought into operation by the 99%. No single facet of existence is accidental. Each creature has its own part to play towards one great purpose. Progress is controlled and guided by many souls. Part of the process of growth for souls who have become reintegrated is to help others less aware than themselves. Each soul, by agreement, is given specific tasks to do.

Respect for all creatures is an important feature of developing awareness. The knowledge of what each creature is will encourage respect.

I don't want to digress here into a discussion on eating habits but at the same time I can't leave the question hanging in the air. Non-human creatures kill each other to satisfy their hunger for food. Humans kill other creatures for food. (I know both human and non-human creatures kill each other for other reasons too, but these are directly related to awareness levels.) However, it's important to remember that only the physical bodies are involved. It's not a black and white question of right and wrong. Fishermen make their livelihood from catching and selling fish and many others are helped to survive physically by the fruits of their labours. Equally, many depend for sustenance on the proceeds from the raising of animals for eventual selling and slaughter as meat, as many do from the eating of meat. These practices don't necessarily hinder the process of growth; they may help it if done with respect.

The Second Stage

The soul has reached a state of awareness which makes it possible for it to achieve reintegration in one unit. It still has many lessons to learn, however, and these lessons have to be effective, that is, they must heighten the consciousness and awareness of the soul. The primary lesson is that it is one soul and that it has free will. It has many guides available to help it to see what other lessons it has to learn and to suggest options as to how they might be learned. One of the common options is incarnation in a human form in specially selected conditions, environmental and otherwise, which will throw up the types of experiences designed for the learning of particular lessons. Human beings did not physically evolve out of (other) animals although souls evolve through different types of physical non-human forms until they reach the human state, but each non-human state and the human state itself were specially designed by the 99% (the Father) for the development of awareness.

The grand design (I'll call it that so as to identify it; I mean, of course, the grand design of the Father - the 99%) envisaged the materialisation of a physical substance which would reflect in a material form the fluidity and infinity of love. Water was that substance. If you visualise water everywhere without any physical enclosure you will at least have a tangible image of infinity. Water came first and all other materialisations evolved out of it. God (or love) created water and evolved out of it shapes and limits to contain it. Each creature - non-human and human - was specially designed out of water. That's the simple answer to all our beginnings in a physical environment. The process of natural procreation built into the design took care of the multiplication of each species.

If I may digress here again a little, I hope you will now see more clearly the significance of water. Physical life cannot exist without it, as you know. But symbolically, also, you can see its importance. Water is the essence of physical life as love is the essence of spiritual life.

Earth existence is only a part of the second stage. The soul has many options from which to choose, such as life on other planets. It may well choose to have a life on earth followed by a life on another planet, or it may decide against either of these options. Earth is the best school of all from the point of view of shortening the journey to awareness. It places so many restrictions on the spirit that the only way of overcoming them is through increased awareness.

You are already well aware of earth conditions. Spirit life generally, including life on other planets, is not subject to the same restrictions and there is no birth or death. The soul is not housed in a body but retains its etheric form which is the form it has chosen in which to manifest itself as spirit. The soul is aware of its immortality, but it is confined to the vibration of its own level of consciousness, with the result that it does not come into direct contact with souls of higher awareness levels and thus the process of attaining higher awareness can be a slow one. (Help is always available, of course, if requested.) Earth is a great leveller in that respect because the physical vibration is the same for all so that souls at vastly different awareness levels come into frequent contact with each other with resultant benefit for at least some of them.

I referred above to the etheric form of the soul which is a shape on the lines of the physical form but without its material substance. Souls in spirit in the second stage of development appear to each other rather like humans do. The only difference is the heaviness of the earth vibration. The souls also occupy themselves in much the same way as humans do but without the element of physical labour. For the sake of illustration let's take a day in the life of a spirit. He has no physical body, so he doesn't need sleep, so he doesn't wake up, he's already awake. However, he likes the idea of being in bed, so he's lying in bed. He also likes having breakfast so he decides what he wants and as he thinks of the different items of food they are there in front of him. He's in a house which corresponds to the type of house he imagines he would like. He feels he would like to listen to music for a while. He doesn't have to go to the trouble of playing a record or a tape or switching on anything, he can just think of whatever music he'd like to hear and he can hear it. Maybe he has some other soul or souls living with him if they are agreeable to do so. It might be his wife in a previous earth existence, for example, if they are both in the same vibration. They may have a common interest in gardening, or listening to music, or theatre, or reading, or walking, or whatever. All these things are available to them just by thinking about them. They may continue to share the experience of making love, if they want to. To sum up, our friend may spend his day and every day and night (I'm continuing to use the earth time terminology; there are no days and nights in the spirit world) doing whatever he wants to do. He may even want to go and look at what's happening to his relatives and friends on earth and even to try and influence them in any way he can; he's free to do this if he wants to unless, as I said in an earlier session, the people on earth ask their guides not to let any other influences get through to them.

So, if I may repeat myself to sum it all up, at the second stage of development life in spirit which includes life on other planets follows the same pattern as life on earth except that birth and death and all the other physical happenings, such as accidents, illnesses, wealth, poverty, the labour involved in bringing a thought or an idea to materialisation, only apply to earth.

Why then would a soul with any degree of sanity choose an earth life?

And why do souls choose to remain earthbound after they have left their physical bodies? It's generally true that all souls who have been through an earth experience are earthbound for a certain length of time. A mother who has left a husband and young children will continue to watch over them and try to help them. If they are constantly grieving for her she will find herself being pulled towards them and her suffering may be very intense because she cannot make her presence known to them. This is something which may perhaps be overlooked. The suffering of the people left behind is obvious but at least they can share it with each other. The mother knows that she could alleviate both her family's suffering and her own if only she could make contact with them. Sometimes she does succeed in meeting them while their bodies are asleep but they don't remember that in the morning, or if they do they dismiss it as a dream or as wishful thinking. The work being done by mediums in this connection can be very helpful because it can break the strong chain of grief. If the mother is able to establish contact with her family a big burden is lifted from them and from her. They still have to face the vicissitudes of earth life without her physical help but they know that she is there and that they will meet again which is a great consolation to them, while she can allow herself to take stock of herself in her new circumstances and in that process she may begin to be aware of the design which makes suffering an unfortunately necessary but inevitably temporary part of life at her present stage of development. However, the mother may decide that she knows what's best for her husband and children, and for that reason she continues to stay around them day and night. That's one way of being earthbound. Not alone will she interfere with her family's lives but she will also continue to hinder her own progress until she frees both them and herself from her obsession. All earthbound souls are slaves to obsessions.

On the face of it, there would appear to be no good reason why a soul should choose an earth existence with all its difficulties over an apparently much easier spirit existence. However, after what may be a relatively short period of time or a long time (there is no pressure) the soul begins to find itself coming up against its own prejudices or limitations which it has imposed on its thinking. For example, a person - for the sake of identification I'll call him Joseph - who followed a strictly orthodox religious tradition while on earth passes on and expects to be judged by God and then assigned to Heaven or Hell or maybe Purgatory. To his surprise he finds that he is much the same as he was when on earth. He even has a body still although it feels much lighter. He can see his relatives around his earth body; it may take him some time to realise that it is his body and that he in fact "died". He may hover around the scene for some time observing the funeral arrangements, etc., but eventually he will become aware of others whom he knew on earth calling to him or talking to him or simply looking at him. He doesn't hear things in the same way as he did on earth. While the sounds are clear they seem to be in his head rather than external to him. The others appear to be as they were on earth except that they look younger and more vigorous. Soon he is talking to them as he would have done on earth. They take him to one of their houses and the journey seems to be accomplished without any effort. They probably sit around and have tea or whatever he feels like having. He is, of course, perplexed. Can this be Hell? Surely not. Is it Heaven, perhaps? His friends tell him that it is and, as far as they are concerned, that's the truth. He asks them have they seen God and have they been judged. They reply, with some puzzlement, that they haven't but that maybe they haven't been here long enough yet. He asks can he still carry out his religious observances and they answer yes, that everything is just the same. The only thing that surprises them is that others who believed differently to them, heretically in their eyes, seem to be here too– except that, of course, they don't attend their religious services.

With the passage of time Joseph settles happily into a routine which suits his thinking. He has his friends, his religious practices, his hobbies. However, questions begin to niggle at him. Where is God? How come he hasn't been judged? How is it that others whom he regarded as sinners seem to have arrived in Heaven too? Then one day one of his friends tells him he's leaving. Joseph is mystified. What - leaving Heaven! How can one do that? Why? His friend explains to him that he has found out that a lot of his thinking was limited by his conditioning, that he has been living in too superficial a way, that he now wants to learn more and to progress further spiritually. He has decided that he will go back to earth for another lifetime in order to undergo experiences and to learn certain lessons from them.

Joseph has now come face to face with a difficult situation. It looks as if what he believes is Heaven isn't really Heaven at all. And here was his friend talking about reincarnating! This was contrary to what he had been taught in his religion. Surely so many wise and learned churchmen couldn't be mistaken in their teaching? His friend understands his position fully - he has been through it all himself - and he says that if Joseph asks God for guidance about these and other questions that will occur to him he'll be sure to get it; that's what he did.

Joseph's friend leaves and he slips back into his routine. But the niggle has now become more like a shout and one day he decides to ask God for guidance as his friend had suggested. Immediately a soul that he cannot recollect having met before appears before him. He is friendly and helpful and he explains that he has come in answer to Joseph's request for guidance. He says that he will be available to Joseph for as long as he wants him, that he has only to send a mental request to him and he will come. He explains to Joseph that he (Joseph) has reached a certain stage in spiritual development but that he has many other things to learn. With the help of visual images he takes him through many of his previous experiences, including earth lives, and shows him that before he had reincarnated he had set out for himself the purpose of each life. Joseph sees where he succeeded and where he failed. His guide explains to him that there are many things outside of his (Joseph's) perception at present and that he will reach understanding and awareness of them only by freeing himself from the limitations which he had imposed on himself, which in turn could best be done either through a further series of earth experiences with the help of a physical body or by remaining in the spirit world and continuing to learn there; that he would be likely to make faster but probably more painful progress by opting for another earth life and that the choice was entirely up to him; that if he chose to be reincarnated he would be helped in the choice of parents and environment and that the whole process could be arranged by agreement between the prospective parents and himself or, alternatively, he could make his own choice of environment and take "pot-luck" on the parents if he wanted to reincarnate more quickly than would be possible under the other type of arrangement; also that if he chose to be reincarnated he could, if he wished, ask for a soul or souls who had reached an advanced stage of awareness to be assigned to him as a guide or guides and that the guide or guides would work with him before his reincarnation and guide him insofar as he allowed them to during his earth life; that, on the other hand, if he chose to stay in the spirit world, he could attend regular sessions with others who were at a like stage of development as himself and who had also asked for guidance where guides would be available to help them grow in awareness; or he could try another environment, still in spirit form, which would be specially selected for him.

Here it is necessary to digress for a moment to explain that when I talk about a soul being someplace in the spirit world it is not occupying space in the same way as humans do. In fact, the spirit world is all around you; souls continue to live their lives in circumstances which very often seem to be the same as earth circumstances, but they are not anywhere in particular. The place is the mind, if you like, or in the mind, or perhaps more accurately, in the awareness. So spirit life can simulate the conditions of earth or of another planet until ultimately no simulation is needed, but earth is the only planet in which there is materialisation. The only significance in talking about life on another planet is that a soul or souls can be isolated for a specific purpose in a particular type of environment which is dissimilar to the environment with which they had become familiar; other planets are reflections of such types of environment. It is not outside the bounds of possibility that at some stage there will be physical or material existence on other planets such as there is on earth; that depends on whether the earth experiment achieves its purpose without stretching the boundaries of pain to an extent which would be unendurable for human beings.

To return briefly to Joseph: he decides that he will opt for the unfamiliar, the other environment. The particular one chosen for him is the planet Uranus. There is apparently no other life around him. He is, of course, still in spirit form so that he doesn't need any physical sustenance. As far as he is concerned he's on his own. For as long as he can remember he has relied on tradition and ritual and the security of conformity in the living of his life. Now he has none of these things. The hope is that when he eventually realises that all his props are now no use to him he will begin to turn inwards and try to come to know himself. He may find the experience too much for him; if so, he can ask to be returned to his previous situation. On the other hand, if he finds himself strengthened by the experience he may be ready to open his mind to other ideas and to move on to the third stage.

> The abiding impression I want to leave with you of the second stage is that it all happens as part of the Father's grand design of growth in awareness. That part of the experience takes place on earth is immaterial (!). You are spirit and you are you whether or not you are temporarily housed in a physical body.

The Third Stage

This, as I said, is a stage of re-evaluation and reflection. From now on the question of place doesn't arise because there is no materialisation. However, if you want to have some image of place, you can imagine weightless beings with all the freedom and space of air and more besides.

The soul has probably had many experiences on earth and also purely as spirit. It is now open-minded enough to be able to go through them all in detail to see where they were all leading and to assess its present position.

At this stage there is no longer any need for souls to identify themselves in terms of sex. The division of the human race into male and female was desirable primarily for procreation purposes but it also served as a useful means for a soul to acquire varied and contrasting experiences through male and female lives. The etheric body retains its sexual characteristics, but that body has served its purpose after the second stage and it is discarded on entry into the third stage.

I think that the easiest way to illustrate how the transition from second to third stage takes place and what happens then is to continue with the story of Joseph. He has been put into an isolated situation without any of the props to which he had become accustomed. There's nothing he can do but think. The loneliness is difficult at first and many times he's on the point of asking to be taken back to his earlier situation (which he had been assured could be done through a mental request to his guide). However, he perseveres and eventually he begins to analyse his thinking on various issues. He finds that he has been praying to God for as long as he can remember but that he has no concept of God beyond that of an all-powerful, all-merciful, all-just, but hazy figure. There is a strong element of fear built into his idea of God. He accepted without question all that he was taught about right and wrong, sin and forgiveness of sin, reward and punishment. Events since his last physical death initially confirmed him in his beliefs but later threw doubt on at least some of them. When on earth, he had thought of Heaven as being with God, but what he would be doing he had no idea. He had thought of Hell as a place of eternal fire but beyond feeling that he didn't want to end up there he hadn't any image of it. Later he thought he was in Heaven, although it didn't conform to his earthly image of it, vague as that was. Then, later still, he found that it wasn't really Heaven and that he needed to make further progress in spiritual development.

So the long lonely days pass. Then one day he hears a voice saying clearly to him "You are God". Horrified, he puts the thought away from him as being unutterably blasphemous. But a little later the voice repeats its message and it keeps on repeating it at intervals for many days with the effect that, while Joseph still cannot accept it, he cannot avoid thinking about it. Then the message changes to "And so is every soul" which introduces a new dimension and makes the idea somewhat more acceptable to him. This is a major step forward in his growth of awareness. Once the idea takes hold he sees himself and every other soul in a completely new light. He begins to realise his own importance as a soul and also that every other soul without exception is equally important. Once he has fully accepted his place in spirit he is ready for the third stage.

The voice, needless to say, was that of Joseph's guide (who, by agreement between them, was continuing to help Joseph). If the guide had given the second message first Joseph would probably have rejected it. The impact of the first message was so great that, by comparison, it was a great relief to get the second one and, of course, it was all the more acceptable for that. The method used to try to raise Joseph's awareness was particularly suited to his state of isolation; if he went around saying that he was God there was nobody to accuse him of megalomania or some other form of lunacy. His guide was able to judge Joseph's readiness to accept the messages. It's one thing to give a message and another to accept it - which is the reason why there's so much trauma attached to the journey back to full awareness.

There's no dramatic business of stepping over the threshold from one stage to another. All that happens is that the state of awareness changes. This is known to the guides who make arrangements for further development.

Because of the change in his state of awareness Joseph finds that he is no longer in isolation. His first impression is of being surrounded by light. He is not conscious of being anywhere in particular - it's not like a room or a house or any enclosure. He's very comfortable but he doesn't seem to be standing up, sitting down or lying down. Now he becomes aware that the light is really a number of separate shapes. As he becomes more accustomed to his surroundings he sees that the shapes are beings apparently clothed in robes with features similar to those of humans.

I said that the etheric body which is used in the non-human states of the second stage is discarded on entry into the third stage. The etheric body is a reproduction in non-material form of the last physical body used by the soul, or if the soul never incarnated in a physical body it represents its choice of manifestation. At the third stage the appearance or manifestation represents the individual characteristics of the soul, or, more accurately, the individual being that the soul is. The appearance literally mirrors the soul and nothing is hidden. I'll be going into this in more detail later.

Joseph finds that he doesn't have to say anything, that thoughts seem to be projected towards him by the other beings and that they seem to be picking up his thoughts. There's a marvellous feeling of harmony all round him and within him.

One of the beings communicates to Joseph that, if he wishes, he will guide him through this particular stage. Joseph agrees. He finds himself alone with his guide who takes him through his complete history as a soul. This is a comprehensive in-depth analysis and there is no selectivity involved as there was when Joseph had previous earth experiences shown to him at the second stage. There's nothing judgmental about the analysis; it's an objective appraisal and Joseph is now able to look at everything in a detached and dispassionate way. He sees the whole process by which he lost his awareness and the painful journey back to where he now is. Nothing, no matter how apparently small or insignificant, is ignored. He sees that he sank to the lowest levels of degradation, that some of his thoughts and actions could only be described as horrible, that he went through states of pomposity and cruelty and hypocrisy, that he also went through states of deprivation and extreme hardship, that he had many thoughts and performed many acts of kindness and beauty. He observes the pattern of the grand design and how time and time again it is obstructed by his unawareness in the use of his free will but also how time and time again it adjusts itself to his changing needs.

The analysis or evaluation takes a long time as Joseph is of a slow and thorough disposition. The time taken doesn't matter. What's important is that he shouldn't move from any happening without thoroughly grasping its meaning. His evaluation finishes when his acceptance of who and what he is and his place in God is total; in other words, that it's not just an intellectual acceptance but also a feeling one; that he knows it within and with his whole being.

At the end he's filled with wonder at the way in which the design worked in his case and with joy that no soul can be overlooked in its operation. He's filled with an indescribably beautiful feeling of oneness with God, although some sadness still remains that he should have separated himself from that feeling for so long and that so many others still don't remember and experience that feeling.

The Fourth Stage

The soul has now reached a full acceptance of its place in God and a full appreciation and understanding of all its experiences since it began its fall from awareness and of how these experiences fitted into the grand design.

Some souls who have reached the fourth stage choose to go back to earth to try to help others. They themselves have no longer any lessons to learn from the earth experience. At the same time by taking on a physical body and going through the states of childhood and adolescence with all the conditioning involved in that process they obscure their awareness and sometimes they may reach a relatively late stage in their earth lives before the veil of obscurity is lifted. But they always know that they have a particular purpose in life and sooner or later they find it. This purpose is usually a common one for a number of souls only one of whom will reincarnate. The others will act as his guides. The number of such souls on the earth plane has increased considerably in recent years and is now approximately one million. Much care has been exercised in the choice of location(s) for their physical existence. They usually operate quietly and unobtrusively and do not seek positions of prominence in the communities in which they live. However, opportunities are created through which their wisdom–including, of course, the wisdom of their guides–is imparted to others who are ready to receive it or even a small part of it.

Souls at the fourth stage also operate as guides to all other souls in lower vibrations who have asked for guides. One human being may have a number of guides, so obviously the guides occupy themselves in other ways also, while they are, of course, always available to help the person being guided.

Perhaps it would be helpful if I first outlined the system by which guidance works and then went on to say something about the other ways in which souls at the fourth stage occupy themselves.

A soul decides to reincarnate. His particular purpose is, say, to learn the virtue of tolerance. He accordingly chooses an environment in which he will meet many different types of people with strongly contrasting opinions. His guide or guides who are working with him in spirit advise him that it would be desirable for him to have more than one guide helping him since he will be faced with a variety of situations and it would be helpful to have guides with him who had themselves coped with similar situations successfully. He accepts the advice. Through a form of mental communication rather like sending messages by computer his guide gets into immediate contact with some souls who have mastered the particular conditions. They all meet and it is decided between them that four of them will act as guides to the reincarnating soul. The guide or guides who have been working with him may or may not be part of the group of guides who will be helping him in his earth existence.

Now the five of them, the four guides and the reincarnating soul, get together. The earth environment has already been chosen. The prospective parents have to be selected. Usually souls who have been through earth experiences together already choose to reincarnate in groups. Sometimes the parents in a previous existence become the children in another or brothers and sisters become parents and children or souls who have been married to each other choose to reincarnate in similar relationships or with roles reversed. Sometimes a soul may wish to have a totally new set of earth relationships although this doesn't happen very often and is usually not successful.

At this stage ideally both the prospective parents and child or children are still all in spirit. If this is so they can come together with all their guides and share their plans for their earth existences. It will be the guides' function to help the reincarnating souls accomplish what they had planned to do.

The decision has been taken, the parents and environment selected, the whole group with their guides, including any other souls who may choose to be born to the same parents and their guides, have had preparatory sessions together, the prospective parents move on to earth, the prospective children continue to live in spirit until their time to be born comes.

Now the physical body is being prepared within the mother's

womb.

The soul and his guides work on the body to shape it to the soul's requirements for his particular purpose on earth. While the physical body is in the mother's womb the soul does not normally stay in it until very close to the time of birth; sometimes it does not stay in it during the process of birth and may even decide that the body doesn't suit its purpose - which incidentally accounts for stillborn births. The pressure of the physical confines takes away most of the consciousness of what has gone before although some of it remains with the growing child until it is usually removed by conditioning. This is, of course, part of the grand design; it represents a real growth in awareness if the soul can reach even some of its consciousness of what it is while subject to the physical limitations of earth existence.

If there is more than one guide each will usually have taken responsibility for certain aspects of the soul's development. They work in harmony and each knows automatically what the other is doing. There's always one of them watching over their human trust who normally doesn't remember anything about them or his arrangement with them. Again this is deliberate. If during his human existence he can reach an acceptance of his guides once he is informed about them - and opportunities will be provided for him to be so informed if his guides consider that he has reached a state of development where this would be helpful for him - then he is obviously making good spiritual progress. It's easy to accept a guide if you see him beside you or opposite you; it's not so easy if you don't and if you're subject to the constraints of human respect and all that goes with it.

Most guides still operate within a climate of ignorance of their existence on the part of the human beings whom they have agreed to help. If the human is living a positive life - for instance, if he generally looks on the bright side of things and is at peace with himself - it is much easier for the guides to help him. They can do this by way of suggestion - how often do you hear people saying "The thought just came to me out of the blue"? - or by helping to create a feeling or an urge, "I just felt I had to go there", or by direct guidance while the body is asleep. How many times do people go to bed with a problem and wake up with a solution to it, without any memory of how they arrived at the solution? During a person's waking hours the guides communicate generally through the pituitary and pineal glands. They're a bit like prompters off-stage during a play. If an actor gets too fussed or excited or worried he won't be able to pick up a prompt; if he stays calm and relaxed he will.

What are the guides doing when they're off-duty(!) from their guidance work? Sometimes they're helping more than one person. They're not necessarily doing developmental things all the time. One of the great things about having reached the fourth stage is that one can enjoy being relaxed without feeling any sense of guilt or reservation about it. Just being and enjoying the feeling is a great pleasure. Get-togethers about the progress of the grand design, philosophical discussions, creative projects, communication with others on what might be called a social level are some of the ways in which souls at the fourth stage occupy themselves (all the souls at this stage still in spirit do not act as guides). A creative project may, for example, take the form of a literary exercise or a scientific experiment. All such projects are geared towards helping other souls reach the fourth stage. Much inspirational writing, including poetry, plays, novels, philosophical treatises, has resulted from such creative projects.

Souls who are acting as guides also act as channels for other souls from higher and lower vibrations to get through to human beings. It is, of course, possible for souls at the second stage who are in spirit to get through direct to humans, and many do, but the guides will gladly act as channels if they are asked to do so. Normally a soul from a higher vibration than the fourth will not seek to get through to a human and will send any message he may have through the guides; where a soul from a higher vibration wishes to get through direct to a human he will only do so by arrangement with the guides and the human concerned.

It is sometimes said that guides, because they are in a higher vibration, cannot prevent souls from a lower vibration getting through to humans due to the fact that the lower vibration is closer to earth. That is not so. Guides have no difficulty getting through to humans if the latter don't put up barriers against them. The very fact that the guides' vibration is higher makes it more powerful. Once the guides are asked not to let any other spirit through except by arrangement with the human being concerned they regulate the opening and closing of the centres by which communication is effected and no other soul can open the centres (except the human himself).

A soul can, of course, stay at the fourth stage for as long as it wishes.

Some souls have decided that they will stay at that stage until all other souls have caught up with them. It's entirely a matter of free will; there's no pressure either way. It's hardly necessary to say that by moving on to the higher stages a soul will still be able to help others. Help is flowing from the Father always as the source of the grand design of help.

The Fifth Stage

The second and fourth stages involve a lot of activity. The fifth is rather like the third in the sense that it is again a stage mainly of reflection and re-evaluation.

Movement from the second stage through the third into the fourth is the biggest transition in the process of development. It is very difficult for a soul to accept, in the fullest possible sense of the word "accept", that it is really a part of God with all that that means; once it has reached the state of full acceptance the rest is much easier. It's not possible to move from the second stage through the third to the fourth without such acceptance in every part of the soul's being. Since the acceptance is already there at the fourth stage there's no barrier against movement from the fourth stage to the fifth except the personal wish of the soul. As I have already said many souls have chosen to remain at the fourth stage until all others have reached that stage and it is generally with some reluctance that any soul moves from the fourth stage because there the concept of what happens to one happens to all becomes very much a reality and there is a deep concern that every soul should be given every possible help to reach the level of awareness that the souls at the fourth stage have regained. Normally a soul will not move from the fourth stage until it knows that it will be able to help others at least as effectively as it could continue to do at the fourth stage.

In outlining the different stages I have tried to give as simple a picture as possible of each and in simplifying I have, of course, excluded a lot of detail. Insofar as the fifth, sixth and seventh stages are concerned the outline will have to be brief since I can find no way of giving a full picture which would be within the comprehension of any soul limited by the physical constraints of physical existence on earth.

A soul who moves on to the fifth stage and beyond that will not normally reincarnate in a physical body. It is, of course, possible for it to do so but it is not part of the grand design that it should. However, the design is continually flexible in its operation.

The type of re-evaluation that takes place at the fifth stage is of a global nature. The soul is already aware of, and accepts, its place in God and has completed its personal re-evaluation at the third stage. Now with other souls at a similar stage of development it becomes aware of the whole sweep of the grand design and it is given an opportunity to study it in all its aspects. It can literally see love infusing all life.

The Sixth and Seventh Stages

Having completed the re-evaluation at the fifth stage the soul is automatically at the sixth stage. The sixth stage is really a broadening out of the fourth. There's a big change in the state of being which I can't describe - it's a matter of feeling - but which in any case I wouldn't try to describe as it's one of the marvellous experiences in store for every soul on the way back to awareness. Once the broadening out is achieved the soul is at the seventh stage.

Souls at these stages oversee the grand design. Specific responsibilities are taken on by agreement.

My particular function or area of responsibility, if you like, is to transmit to humans of what I have in such a way as to help them to raise their level of awareness. I cannot, of course, do this without a human agency. Lest you think that you are merely a channel, that's not so; you are a channel, of course, but I'm only giving you the thoughts not the words. If you didn't have the words to express my thoughts I wouldn't be able to communicate at all in the human sphere. Given your acceptance, my task is easy; but you had firstly to accept that it wasn't your imagination playing tricks on you and secondly to make the commitment to put my thoughts on paper and to share them with others, with the attendant risk of forfeiting your carefully-nurtured image of conformity, or at least inconspicuity.

Now, if I may digress here, I'd like to refer to a statement I made recently (not during these sessions) to the effect that I know all the answers. I said that deliberately to provoke thought. Yes, of course, I do know all the answers, but so do you and all other souls. The only difference is that you have lost your awareness of many of them and are now regaining it while I have been fortunate enough to have regained mine. That's all there is to it.

Here I'd like to take up another point about the contrast between the 1% who will have worked their way back to full awareness and the 99% who never lost any of their awareness. Could it be argued that the 1% will then be more aware than the 99% since the 1% will have been through so many experiences and so much suffering and the 99% won't? Full awareness is full awareness and there can be nothing higher than that. An aspect of full awareness is unity; what happens to one happens to all; in a very real sense all the suffering experienced by the 1% was and is also experienced by the 99%. It could, as a counter-argument, be said that the suffering experienced by the 99% individually is greater than that experienced by anyone of the 1% since each soul part of the 99% feels the suffering of all whereas each soul part of the 1% usually only feels his own. However, the only answer is that full awareness is the ultimate equality.

As I have said earlier the grand design was prepared and

implemented by the 99% who have always been at the seventh stage. Energy is flowing from them at all times to all souls at the different stages. Many souls unfortunately block themselves off from the energy by their own anxieties and guilts and tensions. The seventh stage is heaven if you like to call it that.

Since the fall from awareness first happened and during all the traumatic times in the meantime much attention has been given by the Father (the 99%) to the development and implementation of the grand design. You have heard it said that everything comes from the Father; that is literally true. For purposes of illustration it is helpful to think of the stages in vertical terms with energy flowing constantly from the top right down through all the souls at every stage with no chance of even one soul being overlooked in any way.

But what's the seventh stage - heaven-really like? Well, for a start, try to imagine a state of being in which there's no pressure of any kind to do anything, to be anything other than yourself, knowing that every other soul sees you and loves you as you are without pretence and that you do likewise with them. It's difficult for a soul subject to the limitations of human existence to conceive of unlimited freedom of being. That's what life at the seventh stage is. It's not possible to do justice to it with words. It's a feeling that has to be experienced.

I don't want to leave you with the impression that what you're striving towards is a sort of an ultimate nirvana where nothing happens and where the idea of every soul being so happy all the time sounds boring in terms of eternity. Perhaps the best thing I can do is to outline how I occupy myself. I will first give brief details of my life history to try to summarise on the basis of one soul's experience what I have given you about the various stages.

As a slight digression may I say that I have chosen to categorise the stages into seven with the first being the lowest and the seventh the highest because I wanted to show the process of development in an orderly and simple way from the ground up, as it were. But, of course, it doesn't matter whether you choose to call the seventh the first or indeed categorise the stages in a totally different way. All that matters is that you should understand that there is a planned evolutionary progression and that things don't happen by chance.

As I told you, I was one of the 1%. I was attracted by the idea of having power over others and once I got used to the experience of having power I wanted more and more of it. The more I gained power the less respect I had for those who allowed me to have that power. I was one of the instigators of the multiplication of the 1% into parts and, of course, I did it myself. Out of myself I created two parts which seemed to be exact reproductions of me. Everything was fine for a while until I found that I couldn't control the parts. They wanted to reproduce themselves, and did - and so it went. With each reproduction I was diminished and eventually I reached the stage where I was no longer aware of anything. The nearest equivalent in physical terms is a coma or an extreme state of drunkenness or of being drugged. I was brought back through various forms of insect and animal life to the stage which I have described as the second stage where I became aware of myself as a soul. I won't bore you with the details of my human existences. There were 112 of them and through many of them my old obsession with power appeared again and again and was, I regret to say, often satisfied. Fortunately for me, my guides - many different guides - helped me to grow until eventually, about 2,000 years ago, I moved into the third and, shortly afterwards, the fourth stages. From the fourth stage I reincarnated five times during the next 1,500 years. Then I decided that it was time for me to move on to the fifth and sixth stages. Through the love of the Father I have now regained my full awareness and am back where I started having, alas, contributed in no small way to the cosmic pool of suffering.

Incidentally, I would like to emphasise that the fact that I have regained my former status doesn't confer any unusual distinction on me. Most are, and all must be, as I am. If I can get there, anybody can - and I mean that most sincerely (although I don't want to be taken literally about the body part!).

At present, of course, I'm occupied to a certain extent in transmitting these thoughts to you and, as I said, I'm always available for that purpose. I'm in constant communication with your guides and with others about many things including the overall development of the grand design. Here souls meet and communicate with each other on a basis of friendship and love, but that doesn't preclude any soul from having particular friends. I have a number of special friends. We often engage in creative projects which are our equivalents of poetry, plays, novels, painting or music. That's all still possible at the ultimate stage and in a much more satisfying way than at any other stage. We are no longer searching for meaning in life, of course, but we are expressing its beauty and many-faceted nature. I happen to be particularly interested in literary type activities but there's room for every type of interest. There's no sexual identification - so, needless to say, there's no such thing as the resurrection of the physical body - but there is communion between souls in a way which can never be achieved through sexual intercourse. I can see my friends any time I like or I can be alone. If my friends don't want to see me, that's fine. There's never any misunderstanding of any kind. There are no exclusive clubs or groups, and no inequalities even to the slightest extent. That doesn't mean that we don't make fun at each other's expense. Each of us has his own individual personality which gives an endless variety to life and at the same time is a constant source of humour. We don't become totally transformed beings when we get back to the seventh stage; we mature, in a manner of speaking, and realise our full potential, and are free of all pressures. Even though you've forgotten the details you and every other human being and every soul with any awareness know that there's an ultimate happiness waiting for you if you can but find it. The only trouble is that you tend to seek it everywhere but within yourselves which is the only place it can be found in a coming home to the full awareness of your place in God.

AWARENESS

4th February, 1982: During our earlier sessions I gave material on earth being a training school and throwing up experiences which are designed to increase awareness. I agree entirely that to be aware is, amongst other things, to be without the scars of accumulated experience. The path to awareness - full awareness - involves getting rid of the scars; but in order to get rid of the scars one must learn the lessons which life throws up. Learn but not accumulate as a feeding-ground for the subconscious; learn and leave behind.

Insofar as religious practices are concerned I wouldn't like to go further than I did in our session on religion. Souls are at many different levels of awareness. They can be helped in many different ways including the practice of religion - with the reservation that I already made.

In the final analysis nobody can increase your awareness but yourself and only by looking within can you do that. But you can be helped in many ways; and, as I have suggested, constant communication with your guides is, in my view, the best way. Is there a danger that you would use them as a crutch by, in a sense, passing on all your problems to them? No; they will help you to solve your problems in such a way that your awareness will be increased. You achieve harmony with all life. Once you're in harmony you're in your place, free of all others, not interfering with their freedom in any way. If you're out of harmony you suffer from a lack of freedom and you are diminished to that extent. By putting yourself into harmony with all life you allow yourself to be fully open to the spirit which animates all life (God), of which you are a part and without which you could not be. The guides are channels of that spirit, as you are also, and all souls to the extent that they allow themselves to be. To be fully in harmony is to be completely open as a channel of spirit as well as a part of spirit - something like a link in a chain. On its own a link is of little consequence; as part of a chain it has strength and purpose.

PRAYER – II

22nd February: I expected that my views on prayer would be somewhat disconcerting.

Every soul has a complete and absolute right to freedom. Prayer may be an infringement of that right in many ways. For example, a person who prays that he may be successful in a competition for a job is, in fact, seeking God's assistance in preferring him over others; or a person who prays that a girl friend/boy friend will marry him/her is seeking to influence the mind of that friend in a way that might not be in his/her best interests; or a person who prays that another might be converted to a particular way of thinking, such as acceptance of a religious belief, is trying to influence that person's right of choice. The fact that prayers may be said with the best of motives is, I'm afraid, irrelevant; no person has the right to decide what's best for another.

I have already dealt with the question of prayers for the dead (the physically dead). There's nothing I can add to that.

If somebody asks you to pray for him, or if you offer to pray for somebody, towards the achievement of a particular purpose, what, in fact, is happening? He is asking you, or you are offering, to use your influence (with God) in his favour. This may well make both of you feel good but you may, albeit with the best of intentions, be interfering with that person's purpose on earth.

To take an example; suppose somebody is in bad health. You go to visit him and he asks you to pray that his former good health may be restored to him. You are full of compassion for him and not alone do you pray constantly yourself that the burden of illness may be removed from him but you get others to do so also. The man makes a complete recovery and you are all delighted.

Now it may very well be that it's in accordance with the man's chosen purpose in life that things could happen that way. But what if it isn't? Suppose that in opting for an earth existence the man had decided with his guide(s) that he needed the experience of ill-health on a continuing basis in order to grow spiritually. Through the power generated by your prayers and the prayers of others you interfered with the man's chosen plan. He is grateful to you now - but what will he feel on passing into spirit again when he finds that you have contributed to the frustration of his life's purpose, even though he has admittedly asked you to pray for him?

In your own case you will have added to the burden of learning which you will have to undertake in the future because you will not be able to see the effect of your actions until later on and even then you may not be able to accept what you see without having to go through further learning experiences. And what of the others whom you involve in your crusade of prayer?

I hope I have made it clear why I recommended that prayer should take the form of (a) communication with guides who are in a position to act as channels without interfering with any soul's free will or rights or purpose and who will be able to use the prayer in the best way possible towards the realisation of that purpose, and (b) meditation on unity with the Father.

I know I'm being repetitive to the point of being boring on the subject of communication with guides, but there is no way a person living within the constraints of a physical body can see the overall picture in any given situation.

What I have said about prayer can also be applied to healing. I would strongly recommend that healing should only be carried out under guidance. If a person cannot accept that he has guides I would suggest that before he gives any healing he should ask the Holy Spirit to use his efforts in the best interests of all (which achieves the same purpose in a more formal way).

The thrust of what I'm saying is that people with the most unselfish of motives may quite unwittingly be seriously interfering with the grand design of the Father to the detriment of themselves and the people they are trying to help unless they avail themselves of the guidance which has been provided for them as part of the grand design.

APPEARANCE – HIGHER STATES

23rd February: I promised that I would expand on my statement that in the higher states of awareness the appearance literally mirrors the soul.

The physical body is shaped in a particular way. Some bodies are more attractive to look at than others. What is it that constitutes a beautiful appearance? Regular features, a good physique, clear skin, all these things undoubtedly contribute, but above everything else when one goes beyond the superficial impression countenance is probably the most substantial ingredient. There are many examples of people whose physical features are unattractive but who are yet acknowledged to be beautiful, as indeed there are many examples of people who seem to have all the physical ingredients of beauty but who by general agreement are not beautiful. Obviously there is something that comes from within the person which produces or reflects beauty and which seems to be contained in the word countenance.

Imagine yourself in regular communication with a woman who has a severely disfigured face but who is, nevertheless, a most cheerful, positive and admirable person in every way. After a while you are no longer conscious of her appearance and if somebody meeting her for the first time remarked on it to you, you would probably react with surprise since you have become accustomed to seeing her as a beautiful person. What do you see when you talk to her? You see an impression that she by her inner beauty has created and which, in fact, is the reality that she is. The physical appearance is irrelevant.

A typical example is a young mother growing old; her children are rarely conscious of her physical appearance until perhaps illness or infirmity affects her.

As I have said, there is no physical body, or no corresponding etheric body, in the higher states of awareness. What is immediately apparent is the impression that I referred to above, the real self. It is not obscured by any physical cage which is what a body is.

Each soul creates its own distinct impression and is much more clearly identifiable, although in non-material form, than a soul housed in a physical body.

I can't go any further by way of verbal description. You'll have to wait to re-experience the reality to re-learn what you've forgotten.

GOOD AND EVIL

24th February: Good and evil - the polarisation so frequently preached about, talked about, written about.

I already went into this when I said that there was no evil, only apparent evil, and then illustrated that by way of an example. Yet I know that it is a difficult subject so I'm coming back to it again.

The best thing, I think, is to start at the beginning. I have given my description of God and I have explained how expression evolved out of God and how the fall from full awareness happened. It was not ever, is not, and will never be, possible that any soul could lose its divine nature no matter to what extent it may have lost or may lose sight of that nature. This is the first and most important thing to bear in mind; in fact, it is the fundamental fact about all existence and if anybody does not know this within himself or cannot accept it, then the rest of what I have to say will carry no conviction for him.

The fall from awareness, from grace if you like to call it that, introduced a duality into the fallen souls which was never before present in them. The lure of power, the desire to take precedence over others, obsessions which gave birth to all sorts of attendant corruptions, were and are completely foreign to the fully aware soul. This duality has come to be described in terms of good and evil. It is present in every integrated soul which has not yet regained its former state of full awareness.

For me, the words good and evil have been given much too extreme meanings in common usage to express the duality adequately. However, since they are the commonly used words I'll retain them but define them in my terms.

Good is awareness or the state of awareness which each integrated soul has retained or regained or a combination of both.

Evil is non-awareness or the state of non-awareness in which the integrated soul is at any given time.

Within those definitions there is good and evil in every soul, even a highly-evolved soul, who has not yet regained a state of full awareness (the seventh stage as I have described the stages of growth).

Within those definitions, also, there can be no such being as a wholly- evil soul, since the soul on regaining the stage of integration (the second stage) has also regained some of its former awareness.

Obviously there can be no such beings as devils within the commonly-accepted meaning of that word. The only souls who can be placed in that category are those in a low state of awareness who wish to keep others at, or bring others down to, their own level.

What constitutes a good or an evil action may not be at all obvious.

For example, prayer may be good or evil depending on its usage; apparently good works may turn out to have evil results; equally, apparently evil actions may have good results. The traditional concept of what's good is very often mistaken for the very reason that it limits experience and consequently the growth of awareness. It must be remembered that life on earth was designed as a learning experience. Much traditional teaching has concentrated on good being the avoidance of experience ("occasions of sin") which results in stagnation and a tunnelling of awareness and therefore much greater evil than might accrue from the performance of apparently evil actions which may lead to an increase in awareness and, accordingly, good.

Objectively, there are no such things as good and evil in the traditional sense. There is awareness and there are different levels of non-awareness; or, put another way, there is full awareness and there are different levels of awareness leading up to full awareness.

FEAR

26th February: Fear is a condition common to human beings. It takes many forms, for example: fear of the dark, the unknown, superiors at work, teachers, parents, children, dictators, rulers of different kinds, church leaders, clergymen, policemen, authority generally, being thought foolish or ridiculous, notoriety, poverty, illness, punishment both temporal and eternal, cold, heat, being found to be inadequate, not being loved, not being able to love or to show love, loneliness, old age, middle-age, youth, hostility, competition, confrontation, unemployment, employment, being unemployable, not being able to cope with the problems of the day, meeting people, fire, robbery, mugging, rape, intimacy, nakedness, dirt, cleanliness, change, new ideas, idleness, drunkenness, drugs, promiscuity, nonconformity, anger, insects, animals, crowds, open spaces, heights, enclosed spaces, senility, baldness, wrinkles, sleeplessness, dreams, falling, drowning, choking, travel, meeting prominent people or people who occupy important public positions, the future, God, sin, unworthiness, frigidity, impotence, unattractiveness, being considered mean, accidents, failure, unacceptance, unpopularity, gambling, unhappiness, enjoyment, pain, celibacy, marriage, sexual intercourse, masturbation, contraception, abortion, adoption, fosterage, bankruptcy, dying, death, blasphemy, irreverence, independence, dependence, children not being successful or breaking with tradition, shame, embarrassment, dullness, loss of liberty, war, Satan, devils, ostracism, rejection, loss of status, infirmity, loss of control, criticism, hunger, childlessness.

It is unlikely that there is any human being, or that there has ever been a human being, who has not known fear.

Fear is, of course, an emotional condition rooted in the

subconscious.

It is a learned condition stored in a memory bank which is essentially what the subconscious is. For instance, a child is taught that if he doesn't behave in a certain way in a given situation he will be punished. When that situation recurs he remembers the punishment and its association with the situation, which creates fear in him; this is an automatic response from his subconscious mind.

The human experience produces many occasions of fear (and, of course, many people use fear as a means of controlling others both institutionally and personally). If the soul can overcome fear while being daily subjected to such occasions it will have derived great benefit from its earth existence. It's no easy task, I know, but yet, as with everything, there's a simple answer.

You are a spirit being, part of God. There is no other spirit being greater or lesser than you; all are equal in God. God is perfect, infinite and eternal. Therefore you are perfect, infinite and eternal. Therefore you are indestructible and your condition of apparent imperfection is only temporary (you are trying to regain your awareness of your perfection). Therefore there is nothing to fear.

If you can accept all that you might still find yourself with fear of certain situations or people or things but you will at the same time have an awareness that there is basically nothing to fear which will help you to rise above the occasions of fear and ultimately to exclude them altogether from your consciousness.

CHARITY

2nd March: Charity may mean many things; for instance, giving alms to the needy, treating people in a loving, compassionate manner, visiting the sick, the old, the lonely, saying kind things about people, devoting time and energy to altruistic efforts on behalf of others.

There are compulsory (paying of taxes) and voluntary types of charity.

On a global scale there are programmes of aid for undeveloped countries and special international efforts during times of crisis, such as flooding, earthquakes, famine.

There are also many agencies operating under the umbrella of providing spiritual help where it is thought to be needed.

From the material point of view questions such as the equitable distribution of wealth have troubled people through the ages and, in particular, in this century. Communism and capitalism are often seen as the two extremes of differing opinion on this question.

From the spiritual point of view people individually and as part of organisations wish to share their vision of truth with others and, in doing so, often give up much of what are regarded as the ordinary comforts of life, such as material success, home, family.

If there was no continuity of life, that is, if the death of the physical body was the end of life, planet Earth would be a grossly unjust place with some people living under conditions of extreme poverty and degradation, others vastly wealthy, and many at various stages in between the two extremes; some have all the advantages of modern civilised society, including education, technological aids, comfortable homes, while others are illiterate, primitive, homeless; some have beautiful bodies, others have deformed and ugly bodies; some are born with perfect mental and physical faculties, others are born blind or deaf, or dumb or mentally defective; some have outstanding talents, for example in music, writing, sport, others are mediocre or poor no matter how hard they try. It is strange indeed that so many people have believed for so long that an all - just God, a remote Being, created man and consigned him to one lifetime on earth under totally unequal circumstances, judged him on the basis of performance under those circumstances and assigned him for all eternity to Heaven or Hell as a result of that judgment. Blind faith may have its merits (although I can't see any) - but in what? In whom? Such an unreasoning and narrow view of life is hard to understand.

The logic of the unequal conditions into which people are born becomes apparent when life is seen as a continuing process with earth as a training ground and the possibility of repeated earth lives being open to every soul. In that context life on earth would have to throw up many combinations of experience if it were to provide effective training.

This, of course, is the reality. In order to be given opportunities to increase their awareness it is desirable that some souls should experience hardship and some comfort and all, probably, a combination of both.

Where does charity in its many forms fit into this scenario? This is where I have to become repetitive again. As with prayer (which, of course, is contained in charity), so with charity: Your guides are aware of your life purpose and the life purposes of those for whom your charitable acts or donations are intended and will be able to keep you in harmony with the overall purpose. Communication with guidance coupled with the respect due to each soul as a part of God will ensure that your charity will never be misdirected. Obviously, kindness to each and every soul is an integral part of that respect. This is the ongoing charity which is a commonplace part of daily living and which becomes an automatic process once there is acceptance of the nature of soul; then what I might call formal communication with guidance will only be needed when exceptional opportunities or requests for charity arise.

SIN AND KARMA

3rd – 5th March: In doing these sessions some of the questions under discussion inevitably overlap into each other. This makes it unavoidable for me to be repetitive; I like each session to stand on its own as far as possible and, in any case, repetition serves a purpose.

I have made these opening remarks because I want to talk about sin and karma which are really embraced in the session on good and evil but which, I think, merit isolated consideration since they are important factors in the beliefs of many people.

Sin is regarded as the performance of an act (thought, word or deed), or a series of actions, which offends God. Religious authorities give rulings on what constitutes sin. It is believed that only God can forgive sin but many believe that priests are empowered to do so on God's behalf.

There are many definitions of karma so I'll opt for my own. Broadly, I would define it as the effect part of cause and effect. If you act there is a consequence of your action; the act is the cause, the consequence the effect. All your actions lumped together at any time produce a bank of consequences; that's your karma. It's being added to all the time on the credit or debit side, like a bank account.

Karma is a combination of credits and debits; sin is all debit.

An important distinction between the two is that by an act of forgiveness on the part of God or one of His agents a soul is believed to be freed from sin; on the other hand, a soul's karma is accumulated through its own acts. The existence of a personal God, who is an omnipotent Judge, is central to the concept of sin, but not to that of karma.

As I have already explained in earlier sessions, God does not exist as a separate entity in personal terms. Accordingly, the belief in forgiveness of sin by a personal God is mistaken. The whole concept of sin, with its negative connotations, and forgiveness of sin by a personal God is, in fact, a source of obstruction to souls in the context of life on earth providing a series of opportunities for growth in awareness. If a person believes that if he doesn't commit sin as defined by his religious authority, or that if he spends his whole life committing sin and repents on his death-bed and is forgiven by God, he is assured of eternity in Heaven, then there is no incentive for him to be other than negative in his approach to life. The emphasis on sin as a means of producing conformity in behaviour by stressing things that people should not do, rather than what they should do, has been an effective method of control from an organisational point of view; but life on earth was not designed as an exercise in conformity and indeed is likely to be of no value as a learning experience if lived in that way.

A belief in karma is likely to be more helpful from a growth point of view. The emphasis is on personal responsibility for one's actions which can only be beneficial. But generally belief in karma and cause and effect tends to be inflexible in its approach in that they are seen to be products of an inexorably self-fulfilling law. The sower inescapably reaps what he has sown.

Now I don't want to give the impression that the sower doesn't reap what he has sown. Generally speaking, he does, but not inflexibly. Suppose a man murders another. If he were to reap what he had sown in a literal way he should be murdered himself either in his present or in a future existence, perhaps even by his victim. The Father's design does not work that way, however. The man who committed the murder will be given opportunities to raise his awareness; these opportunities may include his being a victim of murder himself but not necessarily so. The primary objective is to raise his awareness to the point where he sees himself and every other soul in their true relationship in God. The means of achieving that objective are subject to adjustment in the light of his continuing acts of free will; given the existence of free will the design has to be flexible.

The concept of punishment doesn't figure at all in the design. An act of disrespect on the part of one individual towards another can only happen because of a lack of awareness in the person committing the act. Any subsequent hardships which he has to endure are the effects of further acts of free will on his part and/or learning experiences freely chosen by him in order to raise his awareness.

Examination of conscience is a helpful exercise if done positively. Wallowing in guilt is not alone pointless but extremely damaging to the soul's awareness both because it produces a negative effect on outlook and it restricts the possibilities of receiving help from guidance by blocking off receptivity to such help. On the other hand, regular analysis of past experiences with a view to learning from them to the benefit of present and future thinking and behaviour can only increase awareness. By regular analysis I don't mean repeated analysis; I mean analysis of each day's experiences and then finishing with them.

The idea of absolution from sin can also help the soul's growth if it removes the feeling of guilt and produces a positive attitude towards the future. Most traditional religious practices originated with a positive purpose but, as is common with organisations as they grow in size, the negative deterrent side of things began to be more and more emphasised in order to produce a minimum common standard of behaviour.

CHANGE

8th – 11th March: Change is a feature of life. The pattern of change is obvious in nature with leaves falling and growing, flowers withering and blooming, season succeeding season, sunshine following rain. It is also obvious in some ways where human beings are concerned; for example, babies growing, physical development and decline, movement from one dwelling-place to another, taking up employment, transferring from one job to another, marriage, retirement, physical death. But change is affecting human beings every day in somewhat less obvious ways; for example, forming of opinions, reading habits, hobbies, environmental developments, religious practices, travelling conditions, inflation, growth in technology, manner of dress, political developments, laws, social movements.

It is commonly believed that as people grow older they are more resistant to change. Various reasons are postulated for this, such as hardening of attitudes, fear of loss of status, the security of the known against the unknown, physical incapacity, doubts about ability to compete or to cope, apathy, a perceived need to protect positions and possessions.

It is, of course, part of the grand design that life on earth should throw up a continuing pattern of change and, as a result, daily challenges to people the overcoming of which in a positive way will help them to achieve growth in awareness.

But how does one know whether one is receptive to change, whether one has an open mind or a closed mind? Consider your own case. You adopt a flexible approach to every issue that comes within the ambit of your reading, discussion or decision-making, and you therefore regard yourself as being open-minded. You have arrived at a philosophy of living which is based on the beliefs that you are a spiritual being, a part of God, that each and every other soul is equally a part of God, that life on earth is a learning experience designed to help you regain awareness which you have lost, and that you have guides, who are evolved souls who have progressed beyond the lessons of earth, helping you through your earth experience. Suppose you have a friend who is deeply religious in an orthodox tradition who argues with you that your beliefs are contrary to church teaching which he outlines, and therefore not alone totally mistaken but diabolically so? How open are you to his arguments? To what extent will they change your beliefs? Or suppose you have another friend who goes along with you some of the way but who says that it is not possible for evolved souls to communicate with human beings, that it is only earthbound souls who can do so because of their proximity and affinity to the material conditions of earth, and that therefore your trust in guides is misplaced. How do you feel about that? You may argue that your friends are entrenched in their views, but so will they argue about you. Do all three of you, in fact, have closed minds - at least in those areas of belief?

If I may carry the questioning a little bit further I'd like you to ask yourself how can you be certain that the thoughts in these sessions are coming from an entity other than yourself? And if you can make certain of that how can you establish that I am at the stage of evolution that I say I am? And even if you can establish that to your own satisfaction why should anybody else take your word for it and perhaps change previously held views because of what you have written down with imported authority from a self-proclaimed evolved entity?

These are all key questions some of which we have touched on earlier but which, I think, it would be well to consider in some detail now.

The process by which you arrived at your beliefs was in many ways an exceptional one with a lot of concentrated training which would have produced an unbalanced effect in somebody less well prepared for it. You have now reached the stage where your beliefs are merged with your being and you would, in fact, have to reject your whole being in order to reject those beliefs. I don't think that's overstating the position. Accordingly, it's not possible for you to accept arguments such as in the two instances I put to you earlier, no matter how sincerely they are presented. All the three of you can do is listen with respect to each other and be true to your own beliefs. That's being neither open-minded nor closed-minded, it's just being - or being true to yourselves, if you want to put it another way.

That's all right insofar as your own personal beliefs are concerned but it leaves the question of these sessions and, specifically, my part in them still to be answered.

It is, of course, undeniable that I'm a self-proclaimed evolved soul - if I'm there at all! But if I'm not there where has all the material for these sessions come from? Your own imagination is the only possible alternative. Why should you suddenly out of the blue get your imagination working at such a prolific rate in a direction which was previously totally outside of your conception of yourself as a writer - and, in the case of some of the material (how the whole process of evolution started), outside of your previous range of interests? Also, as you have found, there are times when material flows through to you, other times when it comes slowly, and other times when it doesn't come at all - invariably, you have found, for good reasons. So, at least from your point of view, there's enough evidence to satisfy you that the material is coming from some source outside of yourself.

Now, even if it were possible for me to prove to you beyond all doubt that I am what I say I am, it wouldn't be desirable that I should do so. In the first place, the proof would be exclusive to you alone and any reader of these sessions would be no more advanced from a proof point of view than he is now. In the second place, my hope is that these sessions will present a clear picture and philosophy of life in all its aspects which a reader will find reaching him in his inner knowing; if what I have outlined in the sessions is correct, then all the material contained in them is already known to the reader and all I am doing is bringing it to the surface of his awareness; if the material in the sessions reaches him in such a way that he knows that it is right for him, then the authorship of the material is of no consequence and, indeed, is irrelevant. On the other hand, if the material is not acceptable to him it doesn't matter either who or what I say I am, because he's not likely to believe me.

Then why did I do my self-proclaiming bit? My main reason for talking about myself in the first session was, as I said then, for reassurance. It would have placed you in an unfair position and it would have been difficult for you to accept the material if you didn't at least have my assurance that I knew what I was talking about. Any later reference which I made to my personal position was by way of sharing, mainly for illustration purposes.

If I'm what I say I am, of course, the argument that only earthbound souls can communicate with human beings doesn't hold water. (I've already dealt with that argument in an earlier session.) Again, I'll have to let the reader make his own judgment from the material in the sessions.

Insofar as change and open-mindedness and closed-mindedness are concerned the reality is that all souls - young, middle-aged and old - are subject to change and are receptive to it in their own way. It is not wise to make a judgment about anybody else; the fact that he doesn't happen to agree with you doesn't mean that he has a closed mind. Each person can only change at his own pace. The views which he holds may very well be those which are best suited to his present purpose in life; he will respond to other views when the time is right for him. It is never a good idea to try to convince another about the rightness of your views; if you have to try you're doing more harm than good. State your views, if you wish. If the other person is interested he will want to find out more; if not, the subject is best left closed.

CONSCIOUS AND SUBCONSCIOUS – II: HYPNOSIS; DREAMS

16th – 19th March: In an earlier session I discussed briefly the conscious and the subconscious mind. I said that the more in balance a person was the less part the subconscious played in his life. In other words, as a necessary step forward in the path to full awareness the subconscious should be eliminated.

All forms of mind control are exercised through the subconscious. The most extreme form of mind control is hypnosis.

There is a lot of confusion about what constitutes the mind, as distinct from the soul, the brain, the memory, or the imagination.

In spiritual terms the mind and the soul are synonymous. The mind is the real person, the source of thought and feeling. The brain is the physical mechanism which the mind uses in its earth life. Memory is the mind's way of remembering things. Imagination is the expression of the mind.

In the earthly sense, the mind is usually understood to refer to mental functioning, whereas feeling is associated with the soul or the body. In the spiritual sense, the fully aware soul is a perfect blend of thought and feeling; the two are merged into one which can be known as mind or soul if a verbal description has to be used. In my reference to the mind I am talking from the spiritual point of view (needless to say!).

As we have discussed in earlier sessions, people try to control others in all sorts of ways–physical, mental and emotional. One way or another all efforts at control are directed at the mind. For example, fear only becomes effective as a means of control when it registers on the mind. But the mind (the soul, the real being) does not know fear - it's an emotion, as distinct from a feeling, and the real being is feeling rather than emotion - so it rejects it as something alien to itself. If the mind is fully aware there is no difficulty because no emotion can reach it. The extent to which it is not fully aware, in other words the extent to which it is subconscious, is the extent to which it is subject to control.

The subconscious is, in effect, a memory bank of accumulated experiences which have been abortive as lessons to be learned and are therefore still undischarged, in a manner of speaking. Recurrences of the experiences, or similar types of experiences, trigger off emotional responses in the inactive (unaware) part of the mind and add to the bank balance.

The subconscious is the source of all problems. (If there were no subconscious there would have been no need for the human experiment.) It's not much good trying to solve a problem without getting to the source of it, it's like treating a symptom rather than the cause of a disease.

How can the subconscious be eliminated? Different ways have worked for different people, including hypnosis. Given the sort of memories that are crowded into the subconscious hypnosis can obviously be a very dangerous practice if used frivolously. But if the purpose is a healing one designed to get at the root of a particular problem hypnosis can be very helpful. What it does best is to short-circuit the identification of areas of the subconscious which are a source of difficulty; it may also by suggestion negate their influence.

As with other forms of healing I would again emphasise that ideally hypnosis should not be used without checking with guidance and without the help of guidance.

I would not favour the use of hypnosis for regression purposes merely in the interests of trying to prove whether reincarnation is a fact or not. There may be damaging effects insofar as the persons placed under hypnosis are concerned. However, if regression is used as a basis for getting to the source of a present problem it can be very helpful; if done under guidance, I must repeat.

The subconscious tends to run riot in dreams. People are often puzzled as to why they have dreams which seem to them to be just a jumble of nonsense. The only significance such dreams have is that they point to a lack of balance in the dreamers - they are out of harmony with themselves and with life in that they are living too much in their emotions; so, if you have dreams like that, relax, tune in to guidance and find out where the imbalance is occurring: in other words, let light shine into darkness, illuminate and eliminate it.

Some dreams have, of course, a definite pattern and are a source of guidance to people, particularly those who are not aware or cannot accept that they have guides to help them. Generally speaking, if a person is in harmony and in regular communication with his guides he will not have dreams - although he may have recollections of astral travelling which tend to be confused with dreams. There's a simple rule of thumb by which you can distinguish astral travelling from dreams; if you remember having talked to people whom you know to be physically dead, or having visited particular places, or if the sequence of happenings is apparently straightforward rather than symbolical, you are remembering your astral travelling which is a regular occurrence in most cases; dreams are usually either jumbled or symbolical. As I have said, the jumbled dreams are products of the subconscious. The symbolical dreams are their guides' way, or one of their ways, I should say, of trying to reach those whom they are guiding; the symbols are an aid to the development of awareness. They may seem to be wasted on a lot of people (as with all forms of teaching). In all cases, however, at some time a spark will ignite and in due course the flame of awareness will grow.

I started off talking about mind control and I have digressed somewhat into dreams, although the subconscious is a connecting link between the two subjects. Mind control is actually a contradiction in terms. The mind (soul) is free and it is not its nature to be subject to any kind of control (by control I mean the confining influence of another or others). While forms of mind control, such as hypnosis, can, as I have said, produce positive results they operate negatively - like poison on poison in an antidotal sense. In my view, the best way to eliminate the subconscious, that is, to restore the mind to its full awareness, is for people, working with their guides, to be brought face to face with their fears and emotions generally in as conscious a way as possible through learning experiences. If they accept that their difficulties are stemming from the subconscious and that they are no more than phantoms of their subconscious then they can face experiences designed to eliminate the subconscious with a learning attitude, and thus a repetition of the experiences will probably not be necessary.

The commonly-asked question "Why do all these things happen to me?" is invested with a healing rather than a complaining significance when viewed in that light.

MEDITATION: THE MATERIAL AND THE SPIRITUAL

22nd – 28th March: If you observe your thinking processes you'll find that random thoughts seem to be going through your head a lot of the time. This is most obvious in meditation when in spite of the fact that you want to empty yourself of thoughts they often keep crowding in on you with no apparent order or logic. How does that happen?

As I outlined in the last session thoughts are a product of the mind.

You have found that when you are absorbed in a particular task or subject you exclude all other thoughts from your consciousness without any difficulty. When you meditate you are inclined to drift into a state of day-dreaming and thus to become prey to the subconscious part of your mind as happens during sleep; hence the jumble of thoughts.

Day-dreaming is variously regarded as time-wasting, harmless, relaxing, escapist, mind-clogging. It is often confused with fantasy which is, in fact, something entirely different; fantasy usually involves an exclusive line of thought in a specific direction, whereas day-dreaming is formless and scattered.

I have to go along with the view that day-dreaming is time-wasting. It may even be worse than that in that it facilitates the spread of the subconscious.

So what's the solution? No more meditation? Meditation is essential towards growth in awareness. I don't mean that it is necessary to sit down or lie down or whatever for a specific period of time each day and meditate, although that may be very helpful. Ideally, the whole day can be a period of meditation through the way in which all its activities are approached.

On the surface there would appear to be good reasons why people have been encouraged to give some time each day specifically to prayer and meditation; the reasons would obviously include trying to ensure that the spiritual side of life is not ignored. Unfortunately, however, the result has been that life on earth has come to be regarded as a thing of separation between the spiritual and material, whereas the grand design envisages no separation but rather that the material side of life should be an aid to the spiritual.

The physical body is material. The reason for that is to restrict the soul (the real being) to particular environmental conditions so that it will benefit from them spiritually. The body needs certain material things in order to survive - basically, food, clothing, shelter. To meet these needs money is required in the modern world. The acquisition of money has often become an end in itself and in that sense can only fulfil a limited aim, since a person cannot take his money with him when his body dies.

Money and the things that money can buy are all transient - and transitional - both in themselves and their ownership. This is an obviously true statement, but it is also obvious that many people have difficulty in relating its truth to themselves, and to a certain extent at least, they let possessiveness rule their thinking. Broadly speaking, society (certainly western society) and its laws are geared towards the preservation and encouragement of the idea of possessiveness.

From the spiritual point of view it makes no difference whether people own property privately or communally or not at all except insofar as whatever arrangement applies to them helps or hinders their growth in awareness. What is particularly important is their attitude to possessions and the extent to which they are free in their minds from possessiveness (of any kind).

It has become fairly commonly accepted that a person advances spiritually to the extent that he renounces material interests. Religious orders who cut themselves off from the world, hermits, people who take vows of poverty and/or chastity, are obvious examples of subscribers to this belief. The currency of the belief has reinforced the separation between the spiritual and the material in people's minds.

The grand design to which I have to keep referring is that life on earth should be experienced, not evaded. The material needs which people have and ways in which these needs may be satisfied were specially included in the design so that life on earth would provide a wide variety of experiences which would help people to grow spiritually. It is quite likely therefore that the person who participates in the hurly-burly of living is in a better position to grow spiritually than the person who cloisters himself off from it.

That brings me back to what I was saying about meditation. The best blueprint I can recommend for living life on earth in such a way as to gain maximum spiritual benefit from it is to ask your guides each morning to help you to use the day and all its experiences to your best spiritual advantage and at the end of each day to assess, again with the help of your guides, the lessons and progress of the day. That's meditation (and prayer, also) in continuous unbroken action. If as part of the day's activities, you find time for specific meditation or prayer, that's an added bonus so long as it fits into the unity of the day and is not regarded as the only valuable activity of the day. I use the words specific meditation because, in my view, all meditation should be directed towards a particular object; in other words, there should be a topic for meditation - such as unity with the Father as I recommended earlier - since meditation in a vacuum only acts as encouragement to the subconscious.

Spiritually no particular activity has of itself greater value than another. Peeling potatoes, typing a letter, digging a ditch or something else can be of equal or greater or lesser value than writing a poem or saying a prayer or looking at television or collecting for charity; value depends on the attitude with which a person performs the activity. Sine each person is a spiritual being, part of God, all his activities are, in any case, invested with spirituality. (As I have indicated in my choice of examples of activities, I mean the word activity to embrace what may be regarded as passive pursuits such as sunbathing or looking at television as well as what would automatically be classified as active pursuits; in other words, each thought, word or deed is an activity.) In essence, therefore, materialism is only an illusion. All life is spiritual and only varies in degrees of spirituality according to awareness.

Unfortunately, a major feature of the separation of the spiritual from the material is that the spiritual tends to have a morose or kill-joy aura around it whereas the material is associated with enjoyment of life. This perception is understandable because of centuries of promulgation of negative dogmas and teachings heavily concentrated on sin (usually associated with material pursuits) and punishment for sin. Heaven would indeed be a joyless place and a place to be avoided if it were to be inhabited by souls at the level of awareness of so many of those who imposed their codes of moral behaviour on millions through the ages!

The essence of spirituality is enjoyment. It is a celebration of the joy of being. The aware soul makes no judgments, moral or otherwise, in relation to others. Your guides are not there to inhibit your enjoyment of life or to condemn you if you, say, drink more alcohol than you can soberly hold. (Your body will probably condemn you enough!) Only you yourself by your own attitude can separate yourself from the joy of spirit (as distinct from spirits!).

Am I then saying that all things and all aspects of life are there to be enjoyed without inhibition? Yes; but it must be remembered that the aware soul always acts with respect towards himself, towards other souls and towards all life and all things; if he is aware he cannot do otherwise.

RANDOM THOUGHTS

29th March: You find that having a specific topic for meditation helps to focus the mind but that random thoughts still keep intruding. How do you stop that happening? Instead of brushing the thoughts aside try observing each thought as it impinges on your consciousness. Hold it steady without reacting to it in any way no matter whether the thought itself is disagreeable to you or not. After a little while it will fade away. Repeat the process with other thoughts as you become aware of them. Soon you will find that thoughts are no longer crowding in on you and that your mind will grow still. Then you can fruitfully meditate on your chosen topic.

After a few meditations done in this way you shouldn't be bothered with random thoughts any more.

If you react to your random thoughts, even by passing judgment on them which includes rejecting them, you will only encourage the spread of your subconscious and thus retard your growth in awareness.

GUIDES – II

30th March – 1st April: As I promised (threatened!) in our session on guides last October I have been coming back to them again and again.

If you accept that you have guides helping you and that you planned with them your purpose in living this earth life it stands to reason that it is desirable for you to keep in regular communication with them. I already outlined a way of doing that. At this stage I feel that it would be well if I elaborated somewhat on the subject of communication with the aim of helping to make the fulfilment of people's life purposes as simple as possible.

What was the idea in providing guides at all? The 99% (the Father) prepared the grand design which envisaged that all souls would help each other. Picture the way back to full awareness as a ladder. The 99% are at the top of the ladder and, in fact, designed and made the ladder; help is flowing downwards from them all the time to the souls on the various rungs of the ladder. Equally as souls move up the ladder they help those on lower rungs as far as possible. As I outlined in the sessions on the seven stages of evolution (as I categorised them), when souls reach the fourth stage - well up the ladder - they have progressed beyond the lessons of earth, while having experienced life on earth, and can therefore be of great help to souls still going through the earth experience. The grand design was formulated because souls weren't able to get back up the ladder, in many cases even to get on to the bottom rung, by themselves. As a soul reaches the stage of awareness of all souls being a unity he will want to stretch a hand downwards (metaphorically speaking) to help others to join him on his rung.

A soul who has not yet reached the fourth stage has not yet mastered fully the lessons of earth and therefore can help others in a limited way only. Hence the idea behind choosing souls at the fourth stage as guides. They can see the full picture.

If souls could climb the ladder on their own there would be no need for guides. Experience has shown that they can't. This is as true of the souls who have climbed all the way back to the seventh stage as it is of those who are at present at the fourth stage or at any of the other stages.

Life on earth wouldn't be possible at all if souls didn't help each other. People have no problem in accepting this at the human level because it is so obvious - since, for instance, all people start their human existences as babies. Yet the idea of help coming from souls not in physical bodies is often unacceptable and even seen to be diminishing in some way; strange, but yet perhaps not so strange because, by and large, people only accept what they see and since, as a general rule, they don't see spirits it's not so easy to accept that they exist.

Why didn't the grand design make things easier so that human beings could see and talk to their guides? Wouldn't it be logical to expect that they would climb the ladder much faster if such communication were possible?

The answer to the second question is yes, it would be logical to have such an expectation, but whether the desired result would be achieved is open to doubt; awareness tends to come about only through personal experience. In any event, the first question is the key one and the answer to it incorporates, amongst other things; the reason why we are doing these sessions the way we are.

I explained how the fall from awareness happened. The use of free will, that most vital and important attribute of spirit, was the central factor. The fall was not a dramatic one but rather a gradual process and realisation of its happening only came according as what was previously possible came to be impossible - for instance, what I might call inter- spirit total communication, in other words, communication which is only achievable between souls at the same level of awareness. In due course communication of any kind between souls at different levels of awareness was no longer desired (as you will have seen happening with human beings) and ultimately the fact that such communication was ever possible came to be forgotten. With the fall from awareness came a residual resentment and suspicion of those who had not fallen which survived and still survive in the subconscious minds of many and form the basis for the non-acceptance or downgrading of spirit communication including, of course, guides. Souls who are controlled by their subconscious are not comfortable with others who are not so controlled.

This is not so readily apparent in the human context; it is one of the advantages of the earth experience that the physical cage serves as a leveller in that it provides a mask for the thought processes and, accordingly, souls of different awareness levels can communicate to a certain extent without resentment on the part of, and to the benefit of, the less aware; I say to a certain extent because the barriers obscuring communication are slow to fall and movement beyond the superficial is a matter of delicate timing.

The 99%, in their wisdom, felt that it would only add fuel to the dormant (because forgotten) flame of resentment and suspicion if open communication with spirit was included in the grand design. Also, it was essential that freedom of will should be preserved - without it full awareness would not be possible. The right of choice is a basic ingredient of free will and consequently had to be built into the design. Freedom to exercise right of choice would be diminished if the way up the ladder was too plainly signposted by those who were already at the top of it or who had already fully or partially climbed it. But, above all, awareness grows slowly and from within; help to be effective has to be unobtrusive and measured to the capacity of the receiver.

Given that guides were built into the design and that their way of helping had to be unobtrusive the best method of providing such help was through the glandular system of the human body. If conditions were right the guides could transmit thoughts in line with what had been agreed with the receiver before he entered into a physical body. All the guides' efforts are directed towards helping the person whom they are guiding achieve what he set out to achieve. There is never any interference with his free will. By suggestion the guides will try to keep the person being guided on course with his life purpose but they cannot (or I should say may not, if they are true to themselves in the state of awareness which they have reached) do more than that. So that's partly why I place so much importance on the development of two-way communication.

If you meditate on a particular problem, having asked your guides to come through to you with advice, how can you distinguish between your own imagination and whatever thoughts your guides may be directing towards you? Remember my definition of imagination? The expression of the mind. And also that I said that the mind and the soul were synonymous? Your mind (you, the real you) is in tune with your guides. (Your subconscious mind isn't.) Therefore, once you have asked for help–again I must stress the importance of asking because it's the expression of your free will–whatever comes through to you in meditation will be from your guides; your imagination and your guides are completely in harmony. So there's no need to worry about whether the answers you get are coming from yourself or your guides.

You can see now in a broader perspective the reason why so much importance is placed on looking within yourself for whatever answers you need; and also why I keep emphasising so much the need to eliminate the subconscious; if you can do that you'll always be in direct communication with your guides.

Why are some people able to see spirits, others able to see and hear them, others able to hear them or feel their presence, and yet so many others can do none of those things? There's a variety of reasons. Many people are frightened of what they regard as abnormal. Many don't believe in existence beyond the physical. Many think of anything to do with spirits as delving into demonology. Many have chosen lives of complete orthodoxy for specific purposes. Many are simply not ready for such manifestations. Ultimately, the answer lies in a person's chosen purpose in life. It doesn't necessarily have anything to do with a person's state of awareness, although conscious communication with guides cannot but be a help in increasing awareness; communication with other souls in spirit may be a help or a hindrance.

What I might call mediumistic communication with spirit can be risky - because it may give free rein to the subconscious both in the medium and in the spirits coming through - if the medium doesn't ask his guides not to let any souls through except by arrangement. There is no risk once the guides are asked to control the communication. After that, the fluency and effectiveness of the communication depend on the communicator and the medium. Once again, communication is greatly helped if the subconscious doesn't intrude.

CONCLUSION

2nd April: I think that this is an appropriate place to end these particular sessions. As I said earlier, my aim was to simplify, and I hope I have succeeded in doing that. I have tried to provide answers to questions which I expect are, or will come to be, of interest to people. Above all, I have emphasised the importance for each person of regular communication with his guides. This, in my view, is the key to growth in awareness in the simplest possible way.

ABOUT THE AUTHOR

Paddy McMahon was born in 1933 in County Clare in the west of Ireland, and has lived in Dublin since 1952. Employed in the Irish Civil Service from 1952 until 1988, he became aware that he and all people had spirit guides–guardian angels–and that we can communicate with them if we so choose. These communications, which began in 1978, have continued, and have inspired him to become increasingly involved in spiritual counselling and lecturing. Paddy's first communications from the highly-evolved spiritual being Shebaka began in 1981.

BOOKS BY PADDY MCMAHON

There Are No Goodbyes:
Guided By Angels - My Tour of the Spirit World

Peacemonger:
More Dialogue with Margaret Anna Cusack

Living without Fear:
Dialogue with J. Krishnamurti

Amongst Equals:
More Dialogue with J. Krishnamurti

A Free Spirit:
Dialogue with Margaret Anna Cusack The Nun of Kenmare

The Joy of Being
Illustrations by Michel

The Grand Design:
Reflections of a soul / oversoul
Selected excerpts from the five volumes

The Grand Design – V:
Reflections of a soul / oversoul

The Grand Design – IV:
Reflections of a soul / oversoul

The Grand Design – III:
Reflections of a soul / oversoul

The Grand Design – II:
Reflections of a soul / oversoul

The Grand Design – I:
Reflections of a soul / oversoul

Printed in Great Britain
by Amazon